I0568966

BUILDING TRUST FOR FIRST-TIME MANAGERS

The New Manager's Guide to Leading a Highly Effective Team, Building Lasting Relationships Through Tough Conversations, and Fostering an Extraordinary Workplace

PRESTON HUANG

❀ Created with Vellum

To all the new manager who want to build a team that delivers...

Introduction

"If you're in awe when shaking someone's hand, you're not the alpha."

As a first-time manager, you do want to be the alpha because it will make the two paramount, inevitable issues you are about to face head-on easier to fix:

1. They (a team) don't trust you
2. You are dealing with a low-trust organization

The first issue is given. Even if you've worked as a team member from Day One; once you get promoted, the situation resets itself. You are now "the boss," and, as you are well aware, there's something universal about employees' animosity toward an authority figure. Former friends that used to "break bread with you" turn into foes overnight. Consequently, such a level of distrust, personal resentment, and defiance immediately affects the team's performance. It's a behavioral pattern of a group you simply cannot avoid.

However, the severity of the second issue is something you need to analyze in the shortest time possible, especially if you are a newcomer and still not familiar with the routines and habits of your organization, your team, and the individuals within. The problem exists; make no mistake. And it is expected of you to fix it – yesterday.

As a rule of thumb, solving these two problems is a tough nugget to crack for a first-time manager, especially in an expected (extremely short) timeframe. However, once you accept the key elements of the trust-building process detailed here, you will start making real progress. In other words, by understanding what drives human behavior in a professional environment, you will successfully identify critical problems within the five capital groups of every organization (Howe, 2012):

- Employees
- Teams
- Leadership
- Products and services
- Clients, partners, and customers.

The cumulative effect will then ensure that the entire process flows naturally and painlessly.

In the years preceding authoring this book, I had the rare privilege to coach and consult an extensive line of managers and executives in different industries on their journeys toward building high-trust organizations. They were all facing the same challenge you are facing now – **reversing inherited zero growth and low profitability with limited experience.**

Without exceptions, their teams were exhibiting dysfunctional and borderline chaotic behavior. Formed cliques and clans caused impaired performances. Sarcasm was the predominant way of expression. The so-called blaming game was on at all times. And hardly any face-to-face communication was occurring.

Looking up the executive vertical, things weren't in any way different. An instated "cult of a corner office" where the blaming game took almost an art form just to avoid responsibilities at any cost; no respect toward traditional values that keep the company's competitive edge; military-grade secrecy and distrust, and continuous enforcement of the false sense of self-worth and positive outlook.

It was no wonder then that complaints were considered routine on the organizational level while employees' arrogance and open animosity towards clients were pushing through the roof. Consequently, their companies were losing customers. There were no signups of new referrals for months, and even the old clients started sending RFPs again.

However, with my help, they all successfully reversed the paradigms and one by one, put their companies on certain growth trajectory paths.

You see, what many top-level executives fail to realize is that a high-trust organization is built from the top down. In other words, trust goes from c-suites and vice presidents via D-level executives and mid-level managers down to low-level supervisors and other employees. Not the other way around.

It is, therefore, imperative to breed executives and managers who are intentional and knowledgeable about building trust within their teams as the key to achieving overall organizational trust.

Here's the problem.

Remember the "handshake" from the beginning? As a first-time manager, you will never get a second chance to make a good first impression on your team. Therefore, once you step into your new role, you want to be sure that you are well-prepared and utterly confident that you can earn the trust of your employees as a prerequisite for your success as the manager.

In turn, this will allow you to build a functional team that never misses deadlines and always over-delivers.

Easier said than done, isn't it?

That's why I'm here.

The journey you are about to take is paved with less-known tips that have been proven to yield exceptional results for managers of all levels and age groups. Based solely on long-time experience and extensive use of studies, this book reveals actionable steps to facilitate trust-building within your team - with added ease.

Subsequently, through improved teamwork and mutual relationships, increased creativity and output, and above all, a high level of employee engagement, you will quickly move to create a supportive, inclusive, and diverse organization that delivers.

ONE

Becoming a Manager

On his first day in a new role, Bruce Russo, a thirty-two-year-old former race driver, found himself in a dire situation. Just a few days ago, when discussing the terms of his new position, he made the promise to his superior, Caroline Diaz, that he would honor the practice of delivering continuous exceptional results established by his predecessor, now retired, Darnell Lewis.

Lewis, through his long-term experience and impeccable instincts of a true leader, completely transformed one of the secondary production facilities responsible for manufacturing products basically from leftovers. In less than a year, he managed to flip the situation and move from generating losses to running a highly profitable operation. "Nothing goes to waste, remember that, Bruce." Darnell would often say to him. "This entire company was built on the principles of maximum utilization of resources and economy in a true sense of that word."

Back then, Bruce Russo was just one of over a hundred workers under Lewis' supervision. However, he did show promising potential from day one. And Darnell didn't fail to notice that spark of brilliance. So he took him under his wings, confident that one day, Russo will pick up where he left off.

That day came sooner than either of them thought possible. And now, only an hour after arriving at the facility on his very first day, Bruce was facing a full-scale riot. Not a good way to start his new career.

It turned out that, once Lewis was gone, the entire system collapsed overnight. And nobody could figure out why. Nobody but Bruce.

He knew all too well that his mentor was running a tight ship and acted more as a revolutionary leader than a manager. That may have worked for Lewis, but there is a profound difference between these two roles, even though they may intersect from time to time.

What exactly is a manager?

Unlike a leader, who is conveying a vision to inspire teams and ultimately build a tribe of followers, the manager, being mainly responsible for delivering immediate results, is having people working for him.

Therefore, a leader is a visionary while a manager is more of an executive, e.g., Steve Jobs and Tim Cook; Bill Gates, and Paul Allen. The former in both examples is a leader while the latter executes day-to-day tasks; hence, fulfilling the role of a manager.

That role has a certain number of primary duties; the nature and purpose of which depend on the executive level.

For example, upper-level management such as CEO, CFO, CTO, etc., is responsible for creating long-term goals and business organizations.

As we are moving down, we are meeting regional managers responsible for interpreting those long-term plans and setting actions to meet the goals defined in those plans.

At the lowest end of the managerial pyramid, there's a team leader, foreman, shift manager, assistant manager, and like. Their job is to see those plans through on the operational level.

What types of managers are there?

Depending on the core nature of their role within the organization, we can identify four (common) types of managers from the top down:

1. **Head managers** – charged with transferring vision and mission to lower levels and overseeing the overall adoption and goal accomplishments.
2. **Operative managers** – responsible for overseeing particular sectors such as marketing, human resources, etc.
3. **Team managers** – running sub-division of a certain sector.
4. **Line managers** - e.g., a foreman or shift manager in a production facility.

In addition to these four types, a company's founder or CEO may choose to instate an XO (from military terminology; means *executive officer*), commonly known as a General Manager who reports to the top executive(s) and delegates specific goals to lower levels. It's the role responsible for accomplishing financial and/or production goals on the highest managerial level.

But it doesn't come without controversy.

The paradox of being a manager

When Bruce Russo accepted his new position, he immediately found himself between two artillery fires.

On one side, there was his supervising executive, Caroline Diaz, a strong and powerful strategist who somehow managed to capitalize on her, almost maternal, way of keeping the things under control. She expects results, plain and simple. And that means pushing the employees to the limit to meet the ever-growing demands, imposed through monthly production plans that she always strives to outpace by at least 5%. After all, the performance of his team is automatically his performance and vice versa.

On the other side, there were a hundred of his former fellow "brothers/sisters-in-arms" with whom he shared everything for these last five years. Only, unlike those times when he didn't have to worry about sick leaves, personal issues that affect individual output performance, and occasional disputes between the workers; now they are expecting him to be their voice and support. In other words, to be there for them and serve not only as a leader and an organizer but as their advocate as well.

From whatever angle you look at the situation, it seems like a mission impossible to reconcile these two diametrically opposite and confronting sets of expectations.

There is only one viable way to successfully tackle this paradox. Either way or another, the team and the supervisor have to trust you and believe that you are working in their best interests. Of course, it is impossible to keep such a sensitive balance at all times. Sooner or later, one side will tip the scale. And the "losing" side will experience the event as a full-scale betrayal -

unless you've managed to form a strong bond with that losing party.

That's yet another reason why you should reflect an image of a strong and confident alpha who knows what must be done. Remember, **it is not necessarily who you are but who they think you are.**

For your employees, you are both a father and a mother. For your supervisor, however, you are the mean, the tool, and the weapon that gets the job done, every time.

As you progress with this book, you will keep stumbling upon bits and pieces that will ultimately teach you how to best maintain this crucial balance. That is to say, you will learn how to handle both the team and the supervising entities.

So, perhaps, this would be a good moment to learn what managers are not.

The common myths about managers

You first need to understand that yelling won't get you far. It may help to raise your voice from time to time to make a point, but generally, people respond better to a calm, reasonable argument than uncontrolled screaming. In fact, it's arguably the single most counterproductive habit of some managers.

Next, you should accept that meeting a plan doesn't automatically mean reaching goals. These are two different things. For example, the plan might project an X number of produced units, but the goal is to reduce injuries, sick leaves, expenses, or blatant wasting of resources. Sure, you met the number production-wise, but a couple of your people ended up with injuries, and you spent 20% more on supplies than you were supposed to.

Furthermore, it is impossible and even unwise to "treat" all employees equally. In other words, you should clarify to everyone that top performers enjoy additional benefits, provided that they are following the organizational rules and standards. Your attitude toward someone you recognize as a rising star will echo through the group.

> *A golden rule in managing mid- to large-sized groups: if you want everyone to hear an announcement, just say it to any worker, and before you return to your office, a bartender across the street will know.*

If there's one thing you want to avoid in the role of a manager, that's micro-managing.

That old "If you want things done, you gotta do it yourself" doesn't really apply here. Your executive days are over when you start losing time like that. As a manager, your job is to look at the entire image. You can't do that if you are standing an inch from the wall half the time.

As you will learn a bit later, it is exactly this level of distrust that plants a seed from which a low-trust organization is born.

Some people falsely believe that, once you get promoted, it is easy to retain the "stars." In other words, they think that, while it is hard to become a manager, once you are there, it is easy to stay.

It's not. Make no mistake about it. The reality is quite the opposite. The slightly higher paycheck you are receiving as a manager means that your responsibilities are now far greater than those you had as a worker. Consequently, it takes less to lose your position than it takes for the worker to lose the job.

Finally, one of the biggest myths and a frequent self-destructing factor is thinking that you must be the smartest brain in the group now when you are the manager. Quite the opposite is true.

A good manager hires smarter and more skillful people in the areas where that same manager is inferior.

It comes down to objective self-reflecting. Ask any successful top executive or founder. They will all tell you that one of the reasons for their successes is their ability to hire people better and smarter than them. It just might be that you've been chosen for this exact reason. After all, if you want the job done, you are delegating it to a person that shows the greatest potential.

Now when we debunked a few common myths about managers in general, how about we explain what sets apart a great manager from a good one?

Chess vs. Checkers

Marcus Buckingham, head of people and performance research at the ADP Research Institute and a co-author of *"Nine Lies About Work: A Freethinking Leaders' Guide to the Real World,"* explains it best:

> *"Average managers play checkers, while great managers play chess. The difference? In checkers, all the pieces are uniform and move in the same way; they are inter-changeable. You need to plan and coordinate their movements, certainly, but they all move at the same pace, on parallel paths. In chess, each figure moves in a different way, and you can't play if you don't know how each piece moves. More important, you won't win if you don't think carefully about how you move the pieces."*

Buckingham conducted massive research a few years back that included some 80,000 managers. One of the greatest findings was the single quality that sets great managers apart from good and mediocre -- the ability and intention to "discover what is unique about each person and then capitalize on it."

According to Buckingham, best-performing managers not only know but also value those unique abilities. They even go further and embrace small eccentricities common for every human being. It is then just a matter of integrating each individual into an overall plan.

This is also where another significant difference between a manager and a leader hides.

Unlike the leader, who capitalizes on the universal traits and features of the group to push them forward together, in the bulk and the single line, the manager identifies those individual talents and then transforms them into improved performance. Therefore, managers always tend to emphasize differences to challenge each employee to progress personally and professionally, whereas leaders ignore those differences and focus only on similarities.

A good analogy is military leadership in direct engagement.

A commander capitalizes on the XO's work on each individual soldier. The XO made it possible for the commander to have different sets of highly trained skills at his disposal so he could deploy a coordinated attack using the cumulative effect of all those different talents.

That said, it is clear that there are four main responsibilities for every manager:

1. Assembling the team based on different categories of skills

2. Setting expectations to match the most optimal and correct outcomes
3. Using an individual's strengths to develop a customized motivation approach (instead of focusing on flaws and weaknesses)
4. Matching a job with a person

However, the biggest responsibility- the biggest challenge- is to keep growing personally and professionally. In other words, the learning process never stops because, as a manager, you always have to be one step ahead of everyone else. And in today's fast-changing environment, that means continuous development through seminars, coaching, and, finally, reading applicable expert materials aimed toward expanding your horizons, such as Duhigg's "Power of Habits" and Kahneman's "Thinking, Fast and Slow."

Specialized courses, such as Ken Blanchard's training program for first-time managers, are also the perfect "side-dishes" that add valuable memory blocks and build up the knowledge.

A cumulative effect of continuous learning and reflecting on different experiences (both good and bad) will manifest in your increasing ability to improve your team's performance as well as the individuals within the organization. And the founding block is establishing the trust.

TWO

TRUST IS A NONNEGOTIABLE ELEMENT OF SUCCESS

O n June 6, 1944, first lieutenant Richard Winters, along with hundreds of fellow commandos, parachuted into Normandy behind enemy lines in the wake of D-Day. Unfortunately, due to the heavy fire the transport aircraft were taking, soldiers of the 101st Airborne Division had to jump prematurely. Consequently, they ended up -- dead or alive -- scattered across the area, most of them missing their designated landing zones by miles.

Those who survived the hell storm of anti-aircraft projectiles and bullets that were piercing through the sky that night quickly found themselves in every soldier's worst nightmare – detached from their home platoons and without familiar leaders.

In all that deadly confusion and under constant fire, Winters stepped up and showed initiative. He formed an *ad hoc* platoon from the soldiers he stumbled upon on his way to the rally point. They aimed to launch an immediate attack on German anti-aircraft batteries that were ruthlessly bombarding the marines on the beaches.

That single success added to the joint efforts to break through the Germans' iron defense and ultimately changed the balance of power on the battlefield.

How did Winters manage to organize an efficient team on such short notice?

Decoding trust

One peculiar event occurs during the natural formation process of a team. It happens automatically and on the subconscious level of all included.

At one point, from the initial group of "equals," two will suddenly stand out: a commander and an XO (the equivalent of CEO and General manager).

The group forms an ironclad hierarchy in the single moment when the future "second-in-command" publicly acknowledges the proposed or perceived leadership of a dominant team member. The "second" person acts as a real catalyst for the process.

This is one of the most basic human behaviors that allow us to form tight communities built entirely on mutual **trust**.

As a species, we will exhibit this behavior in every given situation where two or more people are in close vicinity because our brains always tend to determine who is the true alpha of the group. It is a fundamental biochemical process that revolves around the release of a single neurotransmitter – *oxytocin*.

Oxytocin is also known as the *bonding chemical*

This natural body hormone that the brain releases in certain situations determines the level of trust and, therefore, the strength of the bond between two or more people that form a single group.

> *The strongest bond is between a mother and a newborn child in the first hour after the delivery. The event triggers the maximum release of oxytocin in both the mother and the child. This is common for almost all mammals.*

In the experiment conducted by Paul J. Zak and his team, two groups were formed to study the causal relationship between trust and oxytocin release. One group, the senders, was tasked to send an arbitrary amount of money to a stranger knowing that it would triple once a stranger on the other side of the computer received it. The other group, the receivers, was tasked to determine how much of the received money each individual receiver would share with the sender – if any. The senders had no way of knowing whether or not receivers would share the spoils.

Therefore, the conflict of interest was clear: the receiver can decide to keep all the money or demonstrate trustworthiness and share some of it with the sender, whereas the sender can take a leap of faith and show trust in a complete stranger by sending more money.

The initial results proved the proposed causal relationship between trust and oxytocin release

The amount of money a person would receive was in direct correlation with the amount of oxytocin the brain would produce as a result. The larger the amount of money, the higher the oxytocin release and the likelihood that the recipient would share the money with the sender. In other words, by sending larger amounts of money, the sender would demonstrate greater trust, which would incentivize the recipient to share the spoils, thus, denoting increased trustworthiness at the recipient. Hence, the more trust we put in other people, the more trustworthy they are likely to be.

In the next stage, scientists administered synthetic oxytocin into the brains of the participants. This artificial increase in oxytocin levels immediately caused senders to double the amount of money they were sending, hence, further proving the thesis that oxytocin has a determining role in trust establishment.

After running additional tests, scientists concluded that oxytocin is a vital factor in reducing the fear of trusting a stranger while remaining cognitively intact. They also showed that elevated trust is not connected to neural disinhibition[1].

Trust vs. distrust

According to the research done by Angelika Dimoka, trust and distrust activate different regions in the brain, which effectively makes them individual constructs rather than opposites of the single continuum, as some scientists were speculating.

Here's where things get interesting.

The first key finding that the advanced fMRI[2] used in the study showed was that trust is connected with the brain's reward, prediction, and uncertainty areas.

The second key finding is that the two main factors in trust assessment: credibility and discredibility, are associated with the brain's cognitive areas.

Translated, this implies that the same way we can cognitively assess someone's credibility (based on the initial emotional response), we could also artificially induce a sense of credibility at another person or a group since it is a cognitive function (deliberate, premeditated, logically weighed).

But it is not a straightforward process by any means.

Unlike trust, distrust, as a separate construct, activates the brain's intense emotions and fear of loss areas. Also, similar to distrust, benevolence, and malevolence, the two predominant emotional responses in our assessment process are associated with those same emotional areas that reside in our limbic (primitive, original) system.

Now, this is where things get tricky and where we can see why we trust some people more than others or why we sometimes suddenly change our opinion.

If we "feel" benevolence (in a person's actions, communication, and body language), we are more likely to label that person credible, hence, to trust. In contrast, when our increased sympathetic response[3] predicts any kind of potential malevolence, we label the person less credible, meaning that we don't trust that person.

That is to say, when we are aiming to induce trust in our abilities as managers, our actions must first "hit" the emotional part of the brain because that's the first stage in the assessment process. In other words, our team must "feel" benevolence in our intentions to ultimately label us trustworthy.

Since benevolence, as a specific dimension of the whole process, lies in the limbic part of our brain, every instance of our behavior will be taken into consideration in a split-second assessment. Send a wrong initial message, and you could unwittingly trigger a negative emotional response, making the entire trust establishment process exponentially more difficult. Because even though people have a natural (evolutionary) tendency to trust, they can also be wary and cautious, especially if they have fallen victim to some past malevolence – possibly practiced by your predecessor.

But why do we have that innate tendency to trust in the first place?

Evolutionary benefits of trust

Remove trust and you compromise love, friendship, trade, and leadership. – Antonio Damasio

In our beginnings, we were selfish and hedonistic creatures, thinking only about our own well-being and benefits. Then, somewhere along the line, something changed. We could argue when and why, but the fact remains that our predominant hedonistic feature had slowly faded away, enabling us to form elemental groups at first and then, soon after, entire communities.

That original distrust slowly made room for open trust. We started sharing and bonding.

That trust made us collectively stronger because, on your own, you can go only so far. But surrounded by a group of like-minded people who trust you, only the sky is the limit. Driven by that same principle, those initial small communities evolved over time into society as we now know it. All because we've decided to trust other people.

However, that innate desire has its negative side.

Since the decision to put our faith in someone else is predominantly based on a subconscious process in our brains, it is, therefore, susceptible to malevolent manipulation attempts.

It is increasingly easy to deceive the subconscious mind because it is time insensitive and cannot distinguish between reality and illusion, which makes it highly exposed to outside influence. The list of examples of major fraudulent attempts, like the case of Bernard Madoff, who ran the longest-known Ponzi scheme that drove thousands into bankruptcy, is simply overwhelming.

Yet, seemingly against all odds, our deeply rooted desire to trust other people remains intact.

This is because our brains, on some level, still remember those early days of human existence when distrust was an automated initial response. Compared to all the benefits that came with the reversed paradigm, brains are still actively supporting trust. It is a simple weighing of the historical facts that tips the scale in favor of trust and deep bonding.

However, on the individual level, things can be slightly different, and as a manager, you are ought to recognize the signs.

For example, a person who suffered emotional or physical abuse during childhood will more likely have a lower oxytocin output, as Paul Zak proved when he tested Stephanie Castagnier, a known "goddess of greed" of the reality TV show, Apprentice.

Zak showed her a video depicting a child dying of cancer while measuring her oxytocin output.

Unlike most participants whose oxytocin levels surged by 47% while exposed to that same video, Castagnier's oxytocin increased only by 9%.

Zak concluded that such a significantly lower output of oxytocin is most likely connected with the Castagnier's traumatic childhood (her father, a drug trafficker, ended up homeless and heavily addicted and eventually died from AIDS along with her mother before Stephanie finished high school).

As you can imagine, having someone like that on the team can not only complicate but also completely compromise and ultimately ruin your efforts to establish trust with the group, especially if such a person has a degree of influence over the rest of the members.

The underlying importance of trust in management

Research after research indicates that in high-trust organizations, people perform better across the spectrum of different areas and individual responsibilities.

An employee of such an environment will show higher motivation and demonstrate increased productivity, unlike an employee of a low-trust organization whose only interest is sole survival.

The former will commonly feel more confident, while the latter's actions and intentions will be limited and even completely inhibited by the fear that fuels the self-preservation instinct. In such circumstances, managers cannot expect any healthy level of creativity or initiative. And without these two, the overall output of the teams is seriously reduced.

The cause of that fear is, paradoxically, the management itself

Divide et impera

In high-trust organizations, team members know what is expected of them. They also feel free to share information with other teams. The complete opposite is true for low-trust organizations where management nurtures a culture of distrust and fearsome competitiveness among the team members.

Under such circumstances, employees operate in a state of chronic distress. And when a human being is forced to act and respond in self-defense mode, those actions are impaired by a severe sense of fear. That fear is primarily caused by one single (extremely counterproductive) policy: mistakes are brutally punished.

Unfortunately, this is true for a large number of companies even though such a policy goes against the very nature of the human species.

In high-trust organizations, however, management is aware that the only way to learn and progress is through trials and errors. Therefore, team members are allowed to make mistakes and can count on both team and managerial support. Without that heavy burden on their shoulders, it is increasingly easier for them to decide in favor of creativity and thinking outside the box instead of status quo and conformity.

And here is the most significant advantage of organizations that nurture the culture of trust: they are completely immune to changes in leadership because teams are almost completely independent and self-reliable.

This is one of the reasons why first lieutenant Richard Winters could quickly and easily form a unit from a mixed group. By default, soldiers trust fellow soldiers because the military, while strict and utterly disciplined, relies heavily on deep bonds between soldiers. They consider themselves brothers simply because they are trained and taught to trust each other so that, in the event where a unit suffers the loss of its superior officer, members can rebound on short notice under the new leadership.

But achieving such a high level of mutual trust doesn't come without challenges.

Keys to building trust

Today's challenges imposed by the high dynamics of the world we are living in, directly reflect on teams and their managers. In the constant race to meet the increasing demands and ever shorter deadlines, managers tend to "temporarily" disregard or completely ignore the trust-building process.

But since trust is primarily the result of a subjective emotional response and emotions have range, there are several levels of it and that fact has a far-reaching impact.

For example, when trust is low(er), the learning is (proportionally) impeded. Consequently, the overall effectiveness is reduced. In practice, this means that the problem becomes a shelter instead of a quest for a solution.

Therefore, as a manager, you should answer the following questions:

- How trust reflects on teams?
- What behaviors build trust and how to implement them in my organization?
- What tools do I have at my disposal to measure the effectiveness of the trust-building process?

These questions, when reversed, effectively reveal solutions to the main challenges of trust establishment:

1. Once you and every team member obtain a fundamental understanding of trust and how it affects performance, you are one step closer to achieving your ultimate goal – building a high-trust organization.
2. Knowing that sharing and open (uncensored, unpenalized) communication are fundamental factors

that enabled our evolution, you effectively deciphered the most important behaviors.

3. Indicators such as team results, mutual support, and support toward the organization (action-oriented); the level of satisfaction, commitment, and identification with the team (feeling-oriented); effectiveness, an improvement over time, and adaptability to changing conditions (learning-oriented) are all good measurement tools to assess the level of trust between the team members and between the team itself and you as their manager.

Once you dedicate yourself to these three components, you are inevitably changing the paradigm and reversing the otherwise unfavorable situation. In other words, you are actively building a high-trust organization which should be your primary concern.

But to maintain that course and accelerate the process, you, as a manager, need to take the initiative in one critical segment.

---

1. In Psychology, *disinhibition* refers to a lack of restraint manifested in disregard of social conventions, impulsivity, and poor risk assessment.
2. fMRI - Functional magnetic resonance imaging or functional MRI (**fMRI**) measures brain activity by detecting changes associated with blood flow. This technique relies on the fact that cerebral blood flow and neuronal activation are coupled. (source: Wikipedia)
3. Also known as *fight or flight* response.

THREE

How a demonstration of passion and knowledge influence teams

People don't care how much you know until they know how much you care. – Theodore Roosevelt

According to the research published in Harvard Business review, when compared with employees at low-trust companies, employees at high-trust organizations report:

- 74% less stress
- 106% more energy at work
- 50% higher productivity
- 13% fewer sick days
- 76% more engagement
- 29% more satisfaction with their lives
- 40% less burnout

In the 1990s, Apple hit the wall. The market share of this three-decade-old personal computer manufacturer was rapidly decreasing while sales were hitting the historical bottom. The future did not look promising. The working atmosphere was ominous.

Then, in 1996, Apple decided to acquire California-based software and the computer company, NeXT, that was founded by Steve Jobs in 1985, just months after Apple's Board ousted Jobs from the company he co-founded.

Little did they know back then that the acquisition would turn into one of the best business moves any IT company has ever pulled.

A year later, Steve Jobs was reinstated as an interim CEO of Apple. Only two years after that, on May 6, 1998, the company announced the launch of its new product, the iMac G3. It was the turning point for Apple, and the refreshing design of the new Mac proved to be a good call.

Immediately after taking on the executive role, Jobs initiated the reconstruction of the company.

From the technical perspective, he reduced the extensive line of products and instead proposed a new, simplified yet recognizable look for the remaining products company has planned to manufacture.

This seemingly simple move had a far-reaching impact that even Jobs wasn't aware of.

Observed by management and employees, Jobs unwittingly transferred his passion to everyone around him. Pretty soon, the *redesigning* process evolved into a global vision and Apple's working philosophy. And unlike the rest of the IT industry that criticized Job's decision to abandon floppy drives and Apple Desktop Bus connector in favor of then-emerging technology, USB drive, Apple's employees along with the Board did not doubt it for a second. It perfectly correlated with the vision Jobs was repeating over and over again: we (Apple) do not accept the status quo; we are challenging it instead.

In America, only 12.3% of all workers show attributes of passion for work, and Apple's employees are among them. Which, in retrospect, means that almost 90% of the entire American workforce don't give their maximum.

So what do Jobs and other managers of those few successful companies do differently?

Creating a passionate working atmosphere

When a team member is passionate, he or she doesn't experience even the heaviest workload as "job" or "work." Instead, the individual challenges of a project trigger almost childish curiosity that gives birth to the iron determination to find a solution.

Such an employee is willingly working long hours. Overtime is simply perceived as a bonus time to be invested in research and development.

The analogy is a personal hobby. Even though it may require sleepless nights and months of hard work, a hobby is a passion rather than a burden or responsibility. Therefore, a passionate team member perceives the job as a hobby – if you set the environment right; like Jobs did.

The question is, how do you, as the first-time manager, inspire three principal traits of a passionate team member:

1. **Commitment** to the process, team, and organization itself
2. Desire to **quest** and **explore**

3. A tendency to **seek out others** in a search for the solution?

(Also note that the absence of these traits indicates that the passion is fading away)

There are four proven initial steps you need to take to set the proper foundation. These steps are also known as the optimal "icebreakers" for new managers, especially in situations where there are no previously established relationships (i.e. when you are arriving in an entirely new environment).

Together, they will enable you to connect with your team on a more personal level (to a certain, optimal degree) while igniting passion team-wide due to the mirror effect[1]. In other words, the team members will ultimately adopt your passion and experience it as their own.

Therefore:

Remove any policy that prohibits or even penalizes mistakes

It is estimated that, by 2009, almost 160 NASA launches had failed, some of them with catastrophic consequences. Still, despite that, NASA is the first and only space agency that landed a human crew on an extraterrestrial object and safely returned astronauts to Earth.

It is highly unlikely that we would see Neil Armstrong walking on the Moon and listen to his legendary punchline if NASA or the US government had a policy in place that, in any way, discourages mistakes, let alone punishes people for committing them. In fact, some NASA divisions went as far as adopting routine actions that enticed engineers to take increasing risks. When something expensive exploded, large applause would break through a control room.

As we already said, humans learn through trial and error. A baby will lose stability thousands of times before that young brain learns that grabbing a leaf of a nearby plant isn't enough to maintain balance. On average, a driver will wreck at least one car and severely damage another before becoming an expert. A new worker will most likely cause certain losses before getting familiar with the process. But eventually, the baby learns to walk, the driver becomes better behind the wheel, and the worker's precision increases.

Unfortunately, those same babies who couldn't keep themselves on their feet for more than two steps in a row, now in their adult life make every effort to suspend the only system we use in any learning process.

A team member who is afraid of making mistakes is anything but passionate and, therefore, anything but productive. Such an employee has no desire to push the limits or exhibit any of the three traits listed above, for that matter.

Incentivize, nurture (and reward) close, interpersonal communication

Trust is best built in close relationships. Your team will keep showing signs of distrust and, consequently, lower output for as long as they don't breathe as one. And to reach that level, members need to feel the desire to communicate with each other in person rather than sending emails or texts.

How important is that communication in building strong relationships was indirectly demonstrated back in 2002 when Eric Paulos, a researcher from Intel Research Laboratory at Berkeley, conducted a social study to determine the significance of the non-verbal communication cues such as physical touch or visual signs for co-located people (i.e. a quick look to confirm the other person's status).

Paulos concluded that those small non-verbal cues act satisfactorily on their own. In other words, there is no need for further confirmation of the status through verbal communication (or body contact for co-located people). However, these cues only exist in people who have established relationships. And as a rule of thumb, the first step to any real relationship is verbal communication. Therefore, by discouraging this vital human need, a manager or company directly affects overall productivity.

> *For his research, Paulos developed a special wrist-wearing device, Connexus, that was capable of sending and receiving real emotions by utilizing force-sensing resistors, ambient light, heartbeat sensor, and Peltier Junction to transmit actuation (heating and cooling of the skin depending on the type of a message). On April 10, 2015, thirteen years after Paulos successfully used the device, Apple released Apple Watch, which, among everything else, was equipped with those same functionalities while, at the same time, was the first commercial device of that kind.*

I'll use a football team as an analogy. A large percentage of their on-field communication is non-verbal. But for the team to perform high, it is not enough to simply learn the "secret signs." The team leader must intimately know every teammate to send the optimal message to a particular team member since, in any given situation, he is facing multiple choices. Hence, to win the yards, he must choose the best option after assessing the current state and shape of every player. The accuracy of that assessment relies on the level of personal relationships the team leader has with each player.

Encourage thoughts and ideas

Employees of low-trust organizations are rarely taking the initiative. At the same time, they are reluctant to openly share their ideas.

It is a situation similar to when a teacher asks a class to answer a question. At first, not many hands are in the air. But as soon as the teacher establishes a closer and warmer relationship with the class, the number of pupils eager to answer the question exponentially rises.

In teams, especially in a situation where a new manager has been installed, members are reserved and hesitant, just like that classroom full of eight-year-olds. Reticence is normal human behavior that can be witnessed every time we are facing the unknown.

However, in companies, team members may exhibit this same behavior for an entirely different and more ominous reason.

Most managers are ruling instead of leading and managing. This causes employees to keep their thoughts to themselves because history has taught them that "being a smartass" may easily backfire.

It is, therefore, your job to change that bad habit and the best way to do it is to openly encourage team members to share their thoughts without any hesitation and, most importantly, without any fear of repercussion or being ridiculed.

Share some (irrelevant) information from your personal life

This may sound trivial but this seemingly insignificant gesture holds tremendous power in trust establishment.

For your team, you are a big unknown. And when we are facing something we don't understand, we tend to try to decipher the mystery even if it means making things up. Our history is full of vivid stories of events that never took place. Yet, it is not rare for that made-up story to take roots and transform into a paradigm.

Remember, the subconscious mind (that drives our almost every action) cannot distinguish reality from illusion. Once a thought takes root, it tends to grow.

Here's the dilemma.

On the one hand, you want to remain a mystery. On the other, however, you want to get closer to each member of your team. And the only way to achieve that goal is to open up (to a certain degree). But sharing too much from your personal life and the mystery is gone which will have a devastating effect on your future relationship with the team because they will start perceiving you as their equal. For managers, paradoxically as it may sound, there is no greater threat than that.

The trick is to "drop a breadcrumb" from time to time in situations when the atmosphere is relaxed. Those breadcrumbs are details from your personal life **that cannot be, in any way, spun or used against you in the future**. Therefore, refrain from revealing sensitive information to keep the guessing game alive.

Hence, the lesson: **never share sensitive details about your personal life because you never know when they will promote you**. It may as well be the same situation Bruce Russo had found himself into when he took over the management of the same team he was part of just hours ago. If he hadn't been more private about his personal life during all those years before the promotion, the new job would have been far more difficult than it already was because the team would perceive him as an equal. This way, he was still somewhat a great mystery to them all and, as such, was quickly accepted as the new leader since everyone had been witnessing his almost uncanny passion for otherwise dull work from day one.

But Russo also installed one additional practice that "sealed the deal."

Share knowledge by "training" together with your team

In a study done by Blazer and Seiler, researchers were examining changes in shared knowledge and verbal communication through collective training of football players. The data showed that shared knowledge has been increasing over time and with practice. At the same time, both dimensions of verbal communication (overall and orienting) have been reducing.

They concluded that "there might be a relation between the level of shared knowledge and the use of orienting communication."

In other words, the more you train with your team, the less confused they will be. As the collective knowledge is rising, there's less need for the team members to ask for specific pointers. The communication evolves from verbal to non-verbal which serves as an ultimate proof that a manager has successfully established trust with the team.

But there is another dimension of knowledge sharing between a manager and team members Through the process of sharing knowledge, you are effectively demonstrating competence;

thus, further adding to trust establishment and the team's overall passion for work.

In a study that included 35,000 randomly selected workers from the US and Britain, scientists discovered one important pattern: having a highly competent boss has a significant positive influence on a worker's level of job satisfaction.

According to the overwhelming number of opinions, for American workers specifically, "having a technically competent supervisor is significantly more important for employee job satisfaction than the salary" - even when that salary is substantial.

This finding has far-reaching consequences because it effectively cancels the generally accepted paradigm that a manager should demonstrate charisma, a high level of organizational skills, and emotional intelligence to be considered a good leader.

Apparently, nobody asked the workers. It turns out that they respectfully disagree. For employees, technical expertise in the managed field is a predominant factor that reflects (positively or negatively depending on the level of expertise if any) on two important segments:

1. The overall job satisfaction
2. Productivity

If the manager "grew and progressed" in the same company, that fact just adds to the overall positive perception.

On the most basic level, employees assess the level of expertise by asking a simple question: could the manager do my job if necessary? If the answer is positive, then the worker is happier.

And when the worker is happier (even by a small factor), productivity increases (by 12%, according to one study).

By demonstrating passion and sharing knowledge through active involvement, we are slowly building rapport with our teams.

The Final Stage: Building Rapport

In several published articles and even according to some well-known business coaches, mirroring or mimicking people is claimed to have a far-reaching positive influence on building rapport between two or more people.

That may be true in relationships of equal parties. But in a manager-employee relationship, mirroring can only serve as an indicator that the employees perceive you as their true leader. That is to say, you should never attempt to mimic your employees; instead, you should lead them to the point where they are mirroring you and your body language. And that's important to remember.

Building rapport is a sensitive and gradual process that develops over time, especially between managers and teams. There are no "neat shortcuts," as some suggest.

Rapport, by its nature, develops exclusively on an emotional level. That implies the necessity of establishing a connection with the other person. And in this context, the simplest but also the most effective way to do so is to break the routine from time to time and ask more personal questions.

This shows that you are taking a personal interest in an employee, which positively reflects on the impression that the same employee is slowly building about you.

Combined with the culture of openness, transparency, and incentivized creativity, getting personal with your team members will inevitably lead to closer emotional connection and, thus, increased acceptance of your decisions and general leadership.

However, that initiative is a one-way street. In other words, while you will lead an employee to talk about out-of-work personal interests such as hobbies, opinions on some non-work-related matters, expectations, dreams, plans, and similar topics, at the same time, you will make sure not to reveal much about yourself to maintain the healthy level of distance.

For some managers, this is a game they play from time to time. For the others, it comes naturally. Either way, you have to tread carefully to avoid negative outcomes.

With passion successfully rekindled, the next step will be much easier.

---

1. In this context, *mirror effect* refers to mirror neurons activity. This specific type of neurons allows us to experience someone else's emotions as our own. In other words, we can feel the same chemical response just by witnessing someone's deed. For example, the feeling of joy you are experiencing when your favorite team is winning is a direct consequence of the mirror neurons activity. On the most basic level, mirror neurons enable us to perfectly blend in because they allow us to mimic our closest social environment on both cognitive and emotional levels.

FOUR

Set clear goals and expectations

How many times have you heard the, "What's the *matter* with you?"

Well, understanding the complex relationship between our minds and the *matter* is what effectively sets apart goal achievers from failures.

In 1923, a French physicist, Louis De Broglie, proposed a novel theory that particles hold properties of waves. It immediately sent shockwaves throughout the scientific community. Some had real difficulties understanding the concept even after analyzing the data.

De Broglie's hypothesis will later become known as the *wave-particle duality*.

Now, what's that got to do with a) setting <u>clear</u> goals and b) subsequent expectations?

As you will soon learn, everything.

To demonstrate the wave-particle hypothesis, English physicist and physician Thomas Young, developed a so-called *double-slit experiment.*

If you shoot, say, a series of marbles into the board through a narrow vertical slit placed in front, the marbles will leave a distinct and quite expected pattern on the board.

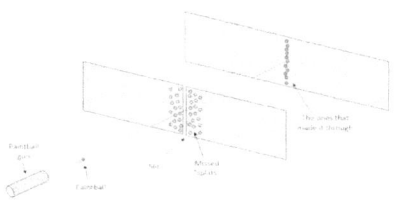

Source: EEWeb (Maxfield, 2018)

Now, if you add another narrow slit and again shoot the series of marbles through both slits, you will end up with two vertical patterns side by side. Hence, the marbles have normal and expected particle properties.

But if you place the board on the surface of the water and instead of shooting a marble, you drop it in the water, the created wave, driven by kinetic energy, will initially go through those slits and then something unexpected will happen. Instead of traveling in a predicted way towards the board (like they did when you had just one slit or when you were shooting marbles through one or both slits), the newly formed waves will diffract and interfere with each other, creating a mash of waves that will hit the board not in two but several different spots; thus, creating several vertical patterns. That's the common property of a wave.

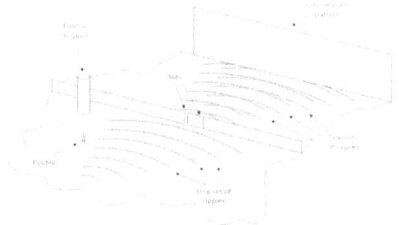

Source: EEWeb (Maxfield, 2018)

Taken to the quantum level (of our thoughts), something truly miraculous occurs *right in front of our eyes.*

If you fire that same marble (matter), this time the size of an electron and in a form of a stream, through a single slit, it will leave that same single band on the board behind. Now add another slip and watch what happens.

The fired matter leaves exactly the same meshed pattern as the wave left back when you dropped the marble in the water. All of a sudden, the matter, the particle, has the properties of the wave. The same will happen if you shoot one electron at the time. After a while, they will create the same wave-like pattern because a single electron leaves as a particle but the moment before reaching the slits, it takes wave properties and goes through both of them and upon exit, interferes with itself to create that wave-like pattern but as a particle again. Mathematically speaking, however, that single electron, at the same moment, went through one slit, through both slits, and neither of them.

Sounds confusing? Just like goals and thoughts are…

It seems that there is something universally elusive about the matter on the quantum level (the level of our thoughts) until…

…we observe it.

In other words, watch the electron on its path, and it will behave again as a particle, leaving two parallel bands on the backboard. Suddenly, all that complex physics and mathematics about waves and particles and duality vanish, and the world starts making sense again. Simply because we saw it. It's like the electron decided to keep its particle properties because it felt it was being watched.

Do you, sometimes, feel like your thoughts are running away from you? You can't seem to remember something important?

Well, welcome to the quantum world of your thoughts. Let them wander around and they will have those illusive wave-like properties. But put them on the paper and visualize them, and the things are taking a surprisingly new and positive term. The world starts making sense again.

Now you know why everybody keeps telling you to write down your goals – to the very quantum detail.

That was something Bruce Russo figured out long before he got appointed to the new role of manager of a somewhat complex production process that involves five different teams. Each team is tasked with a single part of the 4-stage production process that, at the "end of the line," delivers eight different products.

However, to meet the primary goal (5% monthly increment) set by his supervising manager, Bruce Russo had to think four-dimensionally. The production heavily depends on yet another organization that is supplying the Russo's one with raw materials. If they send poor quality, the three dimensions of his top-level goal (maximum utilization, production increase, and quality improvement) suddenly become unattainable.

If he tries to maintain the quality, the percentage of the exploitation of the raw materials will inevitably decrease; thus, affecting one dimension of his primary agenda, consequently making goal-achieving impossible. If he pushes productivity while ignoring the quality, that will have the same negative effect.

Having that in mind, what would you say Russo's immediate goal is?

Correct. He has to develop a strategy and define yet another set of goals to influence the supplier. This just shows the complexity of the job and explains why managers should be innovative, creative, and operate with a touch of Machiavellianism.

However, not even the best quality of the raw materials will help Russo's roof agenda if he fails to a) set clear goals and expectations for his teams inside their three dimensions, b) set realistically attainable goals, c) break down a complex goal(s) to mitigate negative effects, and finally d) keep it moderate in terms of frequency.

Before we explain these four principles, we need to understand what would happen if Russo ignores setting goals altogether. The following would inevitably occur:

- Lack of focus (no clear direction)
- Low motivation (no pressure)
- Frequent distractions (no focus)
- Lack of confidence (the *unknown* factor)
- Low output

The cumulative effect of such a working atmosphere is clear: inability to achieve even the simplest goals.

On the other hand, by setting goals, as numerous studies suggest, a manager positively impacts both the professional and private life of an employee. Goals inspire increased learning, job search success, training transfer, general well-being, physical activity, and fitness-related outcomes (Barends, Janssen, Velghe, Briner, & Rousseau, 2016).

However, those goals and subsequent expectations have to be conveyed to the employee concisely and understandably (preferably in written forms to satisfy the visualization request).

Why does communicating goals and expectations clearly and concisely bears such importance?

A goal is a map. In the most fundamental meaning, if you don't have a map, you don't know where you're going. On top of that, the map needs to be clear and precise, hence, reflecting the reality of the situation. Even a small deviation will most likely derail you off the course.

The same is true for goals. The roadmap must be precise and understandable because you want to avoid any confusion or trigger stress with the *unknown*.

But there is another consideration that just adds to the complexity.

A goal has to be well within the team's capabilities.

The increasing number of meta-analyses show that difficult and challenging tasks have only a moderately positive effect on the individual's or team's performance when compared to easy goals. Some of the studies have been conducted in controlled environments where students were given specific tasks. Others involved active monitoring of the working environment. And while each approach has its positive and negative aspects, both yielded matching results.

If the path scribed in the map follows the route that's beyond an individual's and group's capabilities, the odds are that the goal won't be achieved. If that's unavoidable, the situation requires learning on-the-go.

However, by adding learning to the equation, a manager must either consider reducing the overall complexity of the goal or switch from a specific goal to a more general one (i.e. build 10 feet high wall vs. do your best) to prevent a negative outcome. This request is rooted in basic human biology.

Even though goal-setting, as an intervention for improved steering and increased productivity, commonly induces motivation, hard-to-achieve goals that require additional learning may cause quite the opposite reaction and completely deflate motivation. This is directly connected with the way our body works, as Daniel Kahneman explains.

The main purpose of our brains is to keep us alive using minimal resources. So, the automatic reaction when we come across something extremely challenging (i.e. difficult mental problems such as complex riddles) is to turn our attention the other way. In other words, it is our brain that makes it so easy to give up because hard mental tasks can spend up to 30% of our entire energy reserves which is in direct collision with the brain's primary mission.

Adding to the entire situation is yet another biological fact: we can't utilize the most potent and abundant energy source - fatty acids, due to the blood-brain barrier. For example, if you focus on solving a medium-difficult mathematical problem like multiplying 112 x 11 while running, your brain will instantly slow you down and most likely force you to stop. You can do one or another but not at the same time (not without training at least).

It is, therefore, understandable why the complexity of the goal is, without any doubt, the factor every manager has to include in the goal-setting process.

There is also the *simple task* → *outcome goal* – *complex task* → *learning goal* correlation you should consider. Randomized studies have shown that when an employee is given a simple task, it is better to opt-in for an outcome goal (i.e. result-based) performance-wise. When the opposite is true and the given task is difficult, the more optimal strategy is to define a learning goal (i.e. acquiring a specific skill).

However, if the latter isn't possible, for any number of reasons, the best course of action is…

Further breaking the goal to simplify the execution of every individual milestone.

In other words, making a highly challenging goal simple.

For example, if we set the goal to climb Mt. Everest in the next six months, we won't just scribe the most optimal route and hit the road. Instead, we are going to break the entire expedition to several sub-goals each with its own set of stages or milestones.

In the first stage, for instance, we will only attempt to reach the low-altitude basecamp. But for that to happen, some of our team members perhaps need to go through additional specialistic training. At the same time, we are assessing the capabilities for the next stage where we are aiming to reach the high-altitude basecamp before we attempt to conquer the summit.

As the complexity of the individual sub-goals intensifies, so do the requirements and that fact has to be taken into consideration.

But the last factor is arguably the hardest one to achieve:

Keeping it moderate.

In one controlled study (Schweitzer, Ordóñez, & Douma, 2017), scientists explored the correlation between goal setting and unethical behavior. They wanted to see if goal-setting can, somehow, motivate such behavior. It turned out that it can.

A manager that tends to overuse hard goals while contemplating the achievement with economic incentives is likely to cause unethical behavior by an employee(s) due to the lack of self-control at the latter. This is, to some extent, witnessed more frequently in those who came close to attaining the goal but ultimately failed.

In 2018, as the active fundraiser campaign was nearing its end, CEO of Wallor Wearables, a Texas-based men's fashion company, extended generous monetary bonuses from project managers to the top three most successful affiliates. Forty-eight hours later, the fundraising platform suspended the campaign after receiving an alarming number of complaints (spam reports). Pressured by limited time and the minimum required threshold, several associated affiliate marketers resorted to highly unethical practices and almost caused permanent sanctions. Those affiliates were just short of reaching their goals which caused them to lose self-control and exhibit unethical behavior, consequently endangering the existence of the company.

Additional Considerations

- Generally speaking, long-term goals are less effective in situations that involve learning to attain a goal.
  However, by mixing long-term and short-term goals, as some randomized studies show, an employee can

maintain learned material over a longer period compared to the one that is only tasked with the long-term goals. That is to say, when we are learning new skills, the optimal balance of short- and long-term goals increases the transfer of knowledge in the short run while the long-term goals only produce that increased transfer only after we master the task (Barends, Janssen, Velghe, Briner, & Rousseau, 2016)

- Combining goal-setting with measuring and monitoring of the results has positive effects on the overall performance (Harkin, et al., 2016). In other words, when you provide performance feedback through the ongoing evaluation that correlates with the set standard (of the goal), you should see increased output.

This makes perfect sense when we consider the effect of the *unknown*. If we don't provide feedback, an employee has no way of assessing the progress. That fact immediately renders the employee less motivated, thus, affecting the end goal.

It doesn't, however, necessarily imply a directly communicated review. Employees can obtain the necessary results through frequent and deliberate assessment of progress (i.e. by studying the provided chart). Besides, active monitoring is more likely to further improve the effects if the results are publicly reported (i.e. through meetings, available documents).

- If you can set the goal(s) that somehow correlate with personal interests and values of your team members, the effect on the performance will be measurably stronger. This proves the point that the primary interest of a manager should be building a high-trust organization. A team member who feels the three-way trust (employee-manager-company and vice versa) is more likely to experience every task or goal on a personal level on account of deeply emotional identification with the company's vision and core mission.

Therefore, for the goal to be attainable, it has to comply with three standards:

1. Stems from the top-level goal derived from the organization's core mission
2. Respects the team's overall capabilities
3. Complies with individual capabilities

But there is one additional instance you should have in mind when it comes to goal-setting.

On the one hand, a manager needs to define tangible goals to meet the expectations set by the supervisor or the company itself. On the other and at the same time, managers should actively participate in helping their team members set their personal goals!

Every (perspective) employee has two interconnected agendas: one is reaching the goals set by the supervising manager while the other is achieving personal professional goals (i.e. promotion, learning new skills). It is the role of a manager to support and provide assistance so that these vital interconnecting processes would go as smoothly as possible.

The bottom line is, to ensure that both you and your team attain the goals, design each using the SMARTER rule (Specific, Measurable, Achievable, Relevant, Time-bound, Evaluated, Reviewed).

Most importantly, have faith in your team to reach those goals.

FIVE

Trust them!

The experiment we explained in chapter two shows us one rather peculiar feature of human beings. By showing greater trust through initiative, you are effectively increasing the trust at the receiver's end. Applied to our subject, it becomes clear that it is a manager who should be the initiator of trust.

There are several fundamental reasons for that; all rooted in our primitive behavior:

- Since the manager-employee relation (naturally) implies different statuses relative to the hierarchy (an employee is in an inferior position), it is, therefore, expected that the employee exhibits reserved behavior in any form of communication.
- An employee, almost by default, is leaning toward trusting a manager on the most basic level but needs additional assurance to confirm the instinctive choice. That assurance (or the opposite result) commonly

comes through initial communication and short-term relationship.

- Employees are expecting their managers, given their leadership status, to take initiative in every matter due to the generally accepted leadership paradigm: *leader leads.*
- There is a natural tendency of belonging to the group and getting closer to its leader. However, the speed of the process largely depends on the leader's willingness (even ability) to openly accept a new member. Reaching out first is the best way to build a tribe-like relationship with a "wannabe."

As you will now learn, the latter bears immense importance in building a base of followers rather than team members.

How Trust Affects Rationality

Granted, trust is a two-way street, but it's still the bigger vehicle one that should initiate the trust establishment process by allowing a smaller vehicle to engage in traffic. And here's the unlikely proof.

Gary Alan Fine, American sociologist, and author noticed an unusual -- and rather dangerous -- behavior among the new members of the Minnesota Mycological Society. They would eat the mushrooms a) picked by people they've never met, and b) that they don't recognize by themselves. At the same time, the older members seldom exhibit such behavior.

The conclusion is simple: the desire to belong and be accepted by the group's senior members and, particularly, the leader, is so overwhelming that it almost completely knocks down rational thinking because just one bite can kill a grown human being.

Yet, seemingly against every logic, people are willing to put their lives on the line for the sake of being accepted and trusted.

Again, this feature is connected with the way we are functioning within the group. As an individual, every human being is driven by the innate desire to *fit in*. That can be some brand, alternative group or a group of outcasts, politics, or it can be a company of any size.

Of course, this implies building a powerful culture within the organization, similar to what Google has achieved over time so that the people want to join for emotional reasons rather than existential. HR at Alphabet or Google is receiving thousands of applications each day. It is plausible to believe, considering the public perception of the working environment at Google, that a large number of those applicants are ready to work for free at the beginning just to feel that connection - simply because of the built-in need for belonging to something greater than us.

So how do you, as the first-time manager, capitalize on this feature?

Proof of Functional Reciprocity in Trusting Strangers

An employee, just through the act of employment, demonstrates the most basic desire to belong to the group. But the level of desire corresponds with the employee's perception of the level of trust in the organization. That is to say, in low-trust organizations, that desire may completely void while in high-trust organizations it may escalate and take fan-like properties.

However, given the nature of the relation, an employee is effectively a *trustee* (at the receiving side) while the manager is a *trustor* (at the sending side).

Series of experiments, revolving around the same principle, like the one conducted by Pillutla et al in 2003, show that the reciprocity in trust depends on the level of trust initially invested by a *trustor*. In their experiment, the Trust Game, similar to the one conducted by Paul Zak, Player 1 sends money to the unknown Player 2. However, in this instance, both players are familiar with initial endowments ($10 and $20) of Player 1 and the recipient can even reject the money in which instance both players are losing money. The money triples in value once Player 2 receives it. It is up to the Player 2 to decide how much spoil to share.

Just like in Zak's experiment, *trustees* (Player 2) who received the maximum amount of endowment, shared more money with the *trustor* on account of that initial trust exhibited by the *trustor* (Player 1). But when researchers manipulated the amount and reduced it to just $2, a *trustee* wouldn't share any spoils. That fact leads to the conclusion that recipients have perceived sending less than entire endowment as a lack of trust and instinctively felt the need to reciprocate by not sending anything in return and vice versa.

As Ernest Hemingway once said, "The best way to find out if you can trust somebody is to trust them."

Adam Kipnes from 1495 Group applied this paradigm to the workplace and advocates the practice to give employees easy tasks and let them complete the tasks without any interference. This way, you are "trusting them first" which incentivizes trust establishment while, at the same time, solidifies their belief in you since, in their minds, "you have their back."

However, as Stephen Covey, co-founder of CoveyLink of the FranklinCovey Global Speed of Trust Practice suggests, while you should lead with trust, that shouldn't be a blind trust. Instead, the entire process (proposed by Adam Kipnes) should include clear expectations and accountability. In other words, while handing out the task, no matter how easy or complex it may be, an employee needs to feel responsible for its completion.

That implies a simple conclusion: a receiver of trust, just like Zak's and Pillutla's experiments indicate, <u>expects (and requires)</u> a certain level of transferred risk and responsibility which means that the receiver experiences the given trust as the currency and obligation and; thus, something that has to be optimally repaid.

So, as Covey is implying, giving trust just as an act of formality is not enough. The process needs to be accompanied by transferred values that act as a welcomed and necessary burden. For instance, in the Trust Game, a recipient faces a real dilemma and needs to employ some hard thinking to decide how much money, if any, he or she should return to the sender. In that assessment, the recipient needs to consider several different factors – all connected to the built-in duality (of human beings) between how we see ourselves and how others are seeing us.

Benefits of Trusting Your Employees

It has long been suspected that the level of trust influences the economic results (growth) on both the global and local levels (i.e. a country, a company). In 2001, Paul Zak and Stephen Knack conducted a cross-study to examine the underlying reasons for variations of trust across countries. The study was accompanied by the experiment in which agents transact while facing a moral/hazard dilemma. They may trust the recipients or conduct due diligence first to verify the trustfulness of the recipients.

Long story short, Zak and Knack managed to prove that low-trust environments reduce the investments in both frequency and monetary value.

How is that finding related to the company-level operations?

In business organizations, employees are investing their labor and time in the hope to see the return of the investment through a) monetary compensation, and b) sense of belonging.

Therefore, there is a direct correlation between Zak's and Knack's findings across countries and situations on the local level - in companies. Employees who see reciprocity in returned investment (both instances), will demonstrate:

- Increased engagement (because they feel valued).
- Enhanced level of job satisfaction (caused by the high level of trust and sense of belonging).
- Increased productivity (due to the self-driven incentive for creativity and initiative).
- Improved interpersonal and intrapersonal communication (due to the established trust and lack of any kind of censorship or limiting policies).
- Higher in-team engagement (thus, adding up to the team spirit)
- Tribal-level loyalty (subsequently advocating for you)

At the company-level operations, this improved behavior and subsequent productivity, are directly connected with the company's direct (profit) and indirect (stock price, business evaluation) gains.

One study shows that high-trust culture results in the stock market returns two to three times higher than the market average. At the same time, the turnover rate is 50 percent lower than industry competitors. Finally, a company that nurtures high-trust culture can see increased levels of innovation, customer and patient satisfaction, employee engagement, organizational agility, and more. (The Business Case for a High-Trust Culture, 2016)

Knowing all this, the logical question emerges:

How to Best Communicate Trust

How many companies do you personally know that allow employees to have complete freedom in creating work schedules and/or breaks?

It takes some hard trust in their abilities because every cell in your body screams against such a policy. Years and decades of practice where the manager and manager alone tailor those 8-12 hours at work developed a global habit.

However, the pioneers of the "new wave" or those who dared prove that old habits might not be the best course.

The opportunity to "design" and "organize" work time on your own, makes you happier. And when you are happier, you are more productive. Simple and logical.

One of the reasons for increased happiness and subsequently elevated job satisfaction hides in the illusion that you are in control of your time whereas in the "old system" where your manager was organizing your days, you felt constrained, controlled, and even oppressed.

By nature, we are wanderers and ultimately free creatures that resent any kind of confinement or restraint. Imposed "working hours" are pain points from the first days of the Industrial Age. Yet, it was only in the last two decades that some managers and founders started looking at that issue from an entirely different perspective – the personal one. In other words, how did you feel knowing that someone else – probably someone you don't even know – is tailoring at least one-third of your day, five days a week, fifty-two weeks in a year?

By transferring their desire to the working environment they've created, these daredevils soon started reaping the benefits of their "gamble." A happier worker means higher productivity and a highly elevated tendency toward innovation.

Companies and managers who are practicing this approach are effectively changing the worker's self-perception. He or she does not feel like an employee anymore but like a person – **like a true member of the closed and exclusive group**. With altered perception comes instant trust because the comparison is inevitable. An employee with previous experience simply compares the two systems. Guess which one sounds more appealing?

So, it's not predominantly about the social dimension but rather about assessing the advantages and downsides of each of the systems.

However, as the recent experience from Google[1] shows, managers should tread cautiously with such an implementation. If left uncontrolled or provided with a too wide scope of freedoms, an employee soon replaces a company's mission and well-being with the personal one. At Google, for instance, employees are known for exhibiting a self-proclaimed star level and creating a self-sealed universe inside the company at the company's expense - just because they were having a too wide spectrum of freedoms.

For instance, one employee reports that the riot almost broke loose when Google changed the bus schedules to prevent employees from misusing the food buffet. There was almost a culture of taking out the food and sharing it with the rest of the family. After receiving complaints, Google caved in and restored the schedule.

It's about finding the balance and taking it slowly and arguably the best first step is to have employees create working schedules (organizing shifts). Managed properly and this seemingly odd practice becomes just another bullet point on the manager's delegation list.

On the other hand, if you don't see the likelihood of such implementation, perhaps you should try utilizing the alternatives. After all, this is not a one-fits-all approach.

Different studies draw links between employee's elevated trust and these simple actions:

- Among all the goals you are setting for them, create a truly bold one. They don't necessarily have to reach it but only strive towards attainment. It's yet another challenge that raises the healthy level of cross-department competition. We humans simply love competing and while creativity and freedoms are great motivators, so it compete against "another team."
- Be straightforward in a way that you won't attempt to cover up some bad news either by not communicating or trying to sugarcoat them.
- Invite them to join you every chance you get. It can be a senior meeting or just another brainstorming event where you won't close yourself in the office but "break bread" with them.
- Entice in-team meeting without you where they will be forced to work together in the search for the solution but without your direct interference or help. This builds up the team spirit and just adds to the already established trust base.

- Recognize individual contributions but always keep the balance so that you wouldn't unwittingly isolate members or break the team. It's increasingly easy and comes even naturally for humans to set themselves apart once they "taste the power."
- Be forgiving but have a line they know they can't cross.

These are all practical ways to build trust and, as you could see, each stems from giving trust or trusting your team and every contributing individual member.

However, there are a few instances you should pay special attention to if you don't want to cause a counter-effect and ruin the progress.

Trust inhibitors

If you fail to provide adequate training and development opportunities and limit the chance of working (paid) overtime, that will have a negative impact on the level of trust. (Brown, Gray, McHardy, & Taylor, 2015)

The same study finds that significant reorganization also lowers trust. This is namely because you are changing the developed habits and employees will need time to adjust. So this might only be temporarily provided that you have successfully built a high-trust organization that is, by default, recuperating at a much faster pace than a low-trust one.

But arguably the biggest threat hides in these three mistakes that are, unfortunately, too common:

1. **The infallible leader turns out to be not so infallible.** The most common cause is getting the facts wrong

while sounding over-hyped when presenting the goals, missions, or visions.

2. **The "moral guide" is basically a hypocrite.** This is when you turn out to be the same as the proclaimed adversary

3. **The (constructed) reality breaks or cracks.** This happens when you wittingly or unwittingly destroy the established trust base either with inappropriate communication or wrong messages or if you allow too much time to pass in communication between you and your employees.

The bottom line, lead by example but also, do take note of a) personal achievements and b) failures and make sure to address them properly as it will be explained in the following section.

---

1. Google allows 20% autonomy time where engineers may choose the projects to work on. The downside of that policy was that nobody wanted to work on boring od daunting tasks which, consequently, negatively reflected on projects development.

SIX

Catch People Doing Things Right and Embrace Failures

If we are eager to create environments where people routinely act their best, it's up to leaders to bring out the best in everyone. – Bill Taylor

Bill Taylor, the co-founder of Fast Company, once asked a simple question: what is it about a business that makes it so hard to be kind?

Unlike any other (chosen) situation in our adult life, running a business is rarely connected with pure enthusiasm and a feeling of relaxation like our hobbies are, for example. It is something we *must* rather than something we *want* because we are in constant pursuit of results. And there lies the answer.

In every other area of our lives, results are not the primary concern. Whether we'll drink five beers or only one during those two hours in the nightclub is irrelevant. Will we finish our model tomorrow or in six months is also the least of our problems.

But when it comes to our businesses, that tendency for a casual approach to tasks in hand is suddenly changing.

The pursuit (of results) creates (negative) stress, and when we are distressed, we are partially operating in survival mode. Once in that state, our brains focus on potential threats since that's the basic purpose of the survival mechanism. We do not notice the good because the good is not our current concern. Instead, not only that we are focusing solely on errors, but we are also overreacting to them while completely ignoring achievements.

In time, we develop a habit, and that habit consequently creates a low-trust working environment where mistakes are being punished while achievements meet low to none recognition and/or reward.

The only way out of this vicious and counterproductive cycle is to break the paradigm.

While he was working as a constable back in 1982, Ward Clapham realized something that will haunt him for years to come. Quickly after being assigned to visit local schools, as a part of his patrol duty, he learned that young people -- teenagers and even adolescents -- perceive police officers like him as predators who are taking away kids and their parents. They see them as hunters whose only job is to ambush people.

Clapham became determined to change that disturbing paradigm because it isn't reflecting the true nature of the police force.

He's gotten his first chance to tackle this problem after taking over the command of the third-largest police force in Canada, Royal Canadian Mounted Police in Richmond, British Columbia.

Back then, there was a growing problem with juvenile delinquency. Police officers arresting adolescents was a daily event. With teenagers, the situation was even worse.

However, instead of the stick, Ward Clapham decided to test his theory and use the carrot as often as possible. Soon, he came up with an innovative concept that was a complete novelty to law enforcement. Ward called it *positive tickets.*

According to a new agenda, besides regular policing when necessary, officers would focus on the kids who were "playing nice," meaning that they are staying out of trouble and do little things of kindness every now and then while outside.

Police officers would give a kid a *positive ticket* as a reward. It was either a meal in a restaurant or a movie ticket or a free pass to a theme park. They ended up issuing about 40,000 tickets a year, almost three times the issued citations for various violations involving juveniles.

Was the new concept successful?

Calls involving juveniles breaking the law decreased by 50%. That's some 1,000 adolescents and teenagers avoiding an almost certain visit to the criminal justice and imprisonment systems.

But the most important effect was the change in the perceptions.

Unlike before, when kids would instinctively run away every time a police cruiser would pull into a parking lot, this time, however, they would gather around an officer. Ward Clapham successfully changed the paradigm. Young people were no longer looking at the police as predators and annoyance but as friends and someone to rely on.

Simply because he introduced a new habit – rewarding doing things right.

The psychological effect of reward compared to the punishment

Imagine the following scenario:

You are hiking on the nearby route. Suddenly you feel hunger. With every passing step, the craving for food is increasing. Then, when the situation reaches the critical level, your eye spots an apple tree in the distance. That same moment you feel a small drop of dopamine. Your mood is changing for the better. The anticipation is rising.

As you are closing in on the distance, your brain is continuously releasing new drops of this life-important rewarding chemical. Already in this stage, you are enthusiastic and happier than you were just a few moments ago.

And then, finally, you reach the tree. The ripe big red apple is within your grasp. All you have to do is reaching out and picking the fruit. The intensity of dopamine activation is reaching a critical stage. Serotonin is added to the reward mix. You feel proud of yourself.

However, the tree is placed on the edge of the ravine. And the apple isn't exactly under your fingertips. You do need to stretch out as much as possible.

But the yearning is irresistible. The apple is not just a nice, juicy, round piece of fruit anymore. It symbolizes your success. One way or another, you must pick it. So you reach out, extending your arm to the maximum. Your fingers grab the apple and pull. But the grip isn't optimal. You are struggling to keep it in your hand. Then, the worse happens; the apple slips through your fingers and vanishes in the depths of the ravine, pulling other apples with it because your action caused the tree to swing and, consequently, shed all the fruits.

One little mistake and instead of feeling happy and proud, you now feel sad, depressed, and utterly disappointed. The loss produced a reversed neuronal effect, and your brain immediately stopped the activation of both dopamine and serotonin - the one chemical that makes you feel really good about yourself, also known as the *leadership chemical*.

Just one tiny mistake and everything went down the drain. You are not even considering the option to try your luck with the neighboring tree.

Why?

If you had dropped the apple on the ground next to your feet, picking it up is still achievable. You simply learn from your mistake so that the next time you try, it wouldn't slip through your hand. The "punishment" was insignificantly lower comparing to the reward you felt when taking the first bit. Having bystanders who will cheer you up for your sheer determination to even pick the apple from such a disadvantaged position, further reduces the negative effect of the punishment while increasing the effect of the reward.

However, in a situation where the punishment is greater than the reward, the event will immediately limit your willingness to try again. It is similar to attempting a jump over an extreme distance and failing in the first attempt. The motivation to give it another shot is seriously impaired by the severity of the punishment for the mistake made (pain). But if you succeed and there's someone around to praise your success, the motivation to jump over even greater distance will exponentially increase. The same is true for the failed attempt if someone compliments your daring attempt and helps you figure out how to improve to ultimately reach your goal.

Why reward has such a potent impact on our motivation even if it's simple verbal praise?

In 2012, five Japanese scientists set out to examine the mechanism behind the reward's positive influence on the learning curve. As we now know, any motor skill memory is developed through a two-stage process. During practice (online stage), the memory block is still not complete. It's fragile and can degrade over time. But once it is consolidated offline, it is converted to a stable form, thus, adding to the ultimate mastery of the skill. (Sugawara, Tanaka, Okazaki, Watanabe, & Sadato, 2012)

Three groups were formed immediately after forty-eight participants have finished the sequential task (Group 1: those who received praise for their training; Group 2: those that have experienced praise of other participants; Group 3: those with no praise experience).

Group 1 demonstrated "a significantly higher rate of offline improvement relative to other participants when performing a surprise recall test of the learned (trained) sequence." This led scientists to the conclusion that social reward-related improvements in motor skill memory involve a direct influence on the offline consolidation process rather than just being a feedback incentive.

In other words, the reward doesn't simply motivate us. It is also a required element in our entire learning process mechanism.

A balanced reward system (to increase the effect of anticipation and avoid arrogance)

In every group, organization, or team, there are three types of members (employees):

1. Super-achiever
2. Consistent mediocre
3. Underachiever

Underachieving can be caused either by disinterest or lack of experience. The second group is prevalent and consists of those who are rarely taking the initiative, but their background work is what ultimately delivers results.

Super-achievers are wolves that lead the pack. They are the engine and, in most cases, managers' right hands. In other words, a manager-team communication usually goes through them.

And while all three groups require reward, the second and third are the most critical to focus on – especially because they are frequently overlooked. This is because the "wolves" are already experiencing the rewarding effects since they are a) enjoying the respect of the team and b) serving as communication relays between the manager and the rest of the team which is only adding to the overall effect.

However, the approach should not be unified. That is to say, repeat the same reward over and over again across all three groups, and you'll successfully degrade the positive effect of anticipation. A simple tap on the shoulder and "Atta boy/girl!" have limited effect. To truly create a potent rewarding system, a manager has to break the rules and move outside the box.

How many times has your manager actually looked inside what you were working on?

Hence, the first strategy: *don't be superficial but really connect with your team member by digging into the project and recognizing those small things that say, "Vivian. She is the creative mind behind this piece."*

The important thing is to extend the praise with quality feedback. In that scenario, it means going over the project with the team member and discussing certain issues 1-on-1. The praise is good and welcomed; however, as a manager, at any given time, in any given situation, you have to look further. The praise will boost morale, that's for sure, but the follow-up conversation about the particular parts of the project and that team member's active involvement or role in it, is building trust and helping to solve problems that may not even exist in that stage.

One of the reasons why an employee may reflect mediocrity is the (collective's and self) perception of the underlying importance of the particular task.

In Google, for instance, there are "stars" who are developing self-driving cars and produce an instant awe every time they mention about the project they work on. And then, there are those developers who are removing bugs from Chrome, or Drive, or Gmail services.

On one side, you have self-driving cars that are still long from being globally adopted. A handful of humans have ever been inside the one. On the other, however, annoying bugs in Chrome and Gmail are affecting us right now. So how come we perceive a self-driving car developer a star while completely disregarding even the sole existence of the person who's speeding up our internet browsing?

How would this make the latter employee feel about his job, responsibilities, and the future in the company?

And this is only one example of millions of employees who are executing those known boring and annoying little tasks – without which the entire system would collapse.

It is up to a manager to recognize that underappreciated employee. A simple, honest discussion about the tasks and how they fit in a global vision, accompanied by the old-time favorite, "Atta boy/girl" will definitely change the self-perception and influence the overall output. After all, that employee is also a professional like every other employee. He/she deserves recognition by default.

Thus, the lesson: *don't ignore the second group. Instead, place the biggest focus on them because they are the muscles and brainpower responsible for nearly 80% of the completed products or services.*

What about underachievers? How can a manager spin the situation?

By applying the case-oriented approach where even the smallest achievement can be used in a rewarding process. For example, a new female employee on the production line is still struggling with the technique, but her working slot is simply impeccable. Here's the trick: along with the praise (of her neatness), add accountability. In other words, clearly state that you are expecting the same in the future. That small cue is enough to create a focus and further develop a good habit. And as we know, a habit in one area tends to expand on many. It won't be long before she moves to the second group.

(In case you recognize a complete disinterest even after you engaged the employee, wasting any more energy on that lost cause is futile.)

It goes without saying that you should pay special attention to your "wolf."

The engine of your overall efforts does deserve a certain VIP status. If for nothing else, then for the others to have a benchmark and something to strive for.

Brokerage companies, large hedge funds, investment banks, and alike from the financial sector are almost notorious for their habit of rewarding the most prominent "wolves" with lush monetary bonuses or expensive commodities. The reason why they are using large sums of money that seem unreasonable and unjustifiable to common folk to reward their top executives and brokers is due to the mentality factor – people searching for a career in the monetary sector are interested in making a financial fortune. In other words, only money can produce a satisfying-enough dopamine reward.

The same can be applied to any other industry. Teams' alphas expect privileged status. If they are not getting it, there is a 75% chance that they will quit and seek praise elsewhere.

All these three groups of individual members form a team. And as a team, they expect one additional reward – for their common performance and achievement on the team level.

Arguably the best approach on this level is to accompany the global praise with a thorough demonstration of the **purpose**. In other words, why are they doing what they are doing?

In his book, "Drive," Dan Pink shows how the realization of one's true purpose can have a significant positive influence on performance, "The people in the group reminded of the personal benefit of working at a call center were no more successful in raising money than those in the control group. But the people in the second group, **who read about what their work accomplished, raised more than twice as much money**, through twice as many pledges as the other groups."

Ultimately, plan the group's retreats (i.e. team building, seminars, workshops outside the native company, etc.)

But what are the possible rewards besides just social praise on an individual level?

Don't refrain from rewarding your top achievers with small tokens of appreciation in form of a commodity, a day or two of paid leave, custom-made memorabilia (that reflects a core individual non-professional interest; implies knowing personal details about each of the team members; subsequently building trust!), and even monetary rewards.

While it's true that praise activates the same regions in the brain as monetary rewards, in our current system of living, money has a significant role so occasional bonuses won't hurt.

However, the above-explained reward system only makes sense (and achieves satisfying results) in a psychologically safe environment.

Correlation between a psychologically safe environment and increased effectiveness

Do highly efficient teams make more or fewer mistakes compared to low-performing ones?

The first logic implies that if you don't make an effort, you can't make a mistake. Therefore, you will score low on error test, but your performance score will also be low.

The second logic then implies that the group's high intensity in task processing results in significantly more mistakes.

> *However, in practice, while both of these claims can be true, what commonly separates high-performing teams*

from mediocre or even underachieving ones is the ability of every member, regardless of the rank, to openly speak about issues.

Hence, the third logic: just because a team is seemingly scoring low on error tests, it doesn't necessarily mean that they are not making them. It is more likely that they are just not discussing mistakes.

The most common reason for such behavior is a low-trust organization where the entire vertical of managers nurtures the culture of "horizontal success at any price even to the detriment of others."

In 1986, one NASA engineer became aware of the problems on the rocket boosters. Unfortunately, he couldn't alert the upper management on time. That same day, space shuttle Challenger exploded just 73 seconds after lift-off due to the defective rocket boosters. Seven crew members died. If there was open communication between all levels, it is questionable whether the accident would've happened.

What happens when a manager opens the communication channel and ensures that there is no judgment for reporting errors?

What would commonly be an "individual repairment," suddenly becomes a team effort and activity. (Redford, 2019)

The major difference lies in the fact that, unlike in the closed system where mistakes are discussed between a manager and an individual team member, in a psychologically safe environment, the mistake effectively becomes a global learning tool.

Let's use our apple tree situation one more time.

If every team member attempts picking the apple individually and fails but doesn't report the error, it is reasonable to believe that, in order for the team to learn the right way, every single member must go through the process. However, in the situation where the team is gathered around the apple or where the mistake has been a) reported to the collective, and b) discussed globally, it is logical to believe that at least some members will be successful from the first attempt.

This is only possible in the environment where employees feel free to admit mistakes that don't result in punishment but in a lesson for everyone to learn from.

How to properly address serious mistakes

Some errors are more severe than others; since every employee must be held accountable, a reprimand is inevitable. However, the optimal approach is somewhat different from what most of managers (new and old) are accustomed to.

Ken Blanchard and Spencer Johnson advise one particular reprimand system that stems from the correct start. In their book, "The One Minute Manager," they are proposing a (now tested) 3-phase methodology with each lasting no more than 1 minute.

The process starts with **clearly defined goals for every employee – especially newcomers**. The goal should be simple enough so each of you can review it in less than a minute.

The next step is **praise after a job/task well-done** but it has to occur as soon as possible, ideally right after the task has been successfully completed or a goal achieved. The praise itself should not last for more than 1 minute.

Ultimately, a manager should **spend no more than one minute to a) reprimand an employee over a poorly executed task or a failure to achieve a goal** while b) praising the directly or indirectly connected aspect of the employee's overall responsibilities. This way, the error reporting doesn't create a significant negative effect since the employee has received a social reward at the same time. The latter balances the former. And same as with praise, the reprimand should occur immediately after the mistake has happened or been reported.

> *The analogy is punishing a child for something the child did a couple of days earlier. The measure has no effect, and that's the reason why almost every country has a statute of limitations built in the very core of the judicial system.*

But what about your own mistakes? Should you communicate with them openly? If so, how?

SEVEN

Admit Your Own Mistakes and Share Credit

Tread lightly when admitting your mistakes in front of a team.

The fact: employees exhibit higher trust toward managers that are capable of executing an individual employee's task if necessary.

It is almost a paradigm and the primary method of assessing the competency of the manager. Plus, it is the primary factor in weighing whether or not a manager should be perceived as a superior and; thus, the (respected) leader. In other words, the level of respect your employees will have for you predominantly depends on their perception of your relevant technical skills.

This paradigm should, therefore, always be in the back of your mind when deciding to openly discuss the mistake you've made.

That being said, there are a few reasons why a manager would do such a seemingly illogical thing.

Why would you want to admit a mistake and to what extent?

Word of advice: serious errors that threaten an overall team's effort and goals should be discussed on a theoretical level only. That is to say, employees should perceive it as yet another lesson and presentation. Otherwise, you could undermine your status which will just add to the entire problem.

However, as Glenn Llopis writes in his Inc. article "4 Reasons Great Leaders Admit Their Mistakes," admitting and openly discussing (some minor) mistake can, in fact, **improve the respect you're enjoying among your team**. And he uses a good argument too. Unlike the team members, leaders are expected to take calculated risks on a much greater level. Naturally, that won't always return desired results. So besides just creating an environment of transparency, you are once again using the mistake as a valuable lesson – for both you and your team.

Subsequently, you **lead the way for the rest of the team to open up and admit their mistakes**. Because if they see their leader being flexible and open about own mistakes, they will feel more empowered and motivated to share theirs. The situation, therefore, **adds another brick in building a high-trust organization.**

But should you ever apologize for the mistake even if your wrongdoing inflicted damage to a team's trust base and stability?

The anatomy of an (effective) apology

ELABORATION

↓

ACKNOWLEDGMENT

↓

REPARATION

In simple words, instead of just saying "I'm sorry (for what happened)," one should demonstrate a clear understanding of all the consequences his or her mistake caused and offer a viable solution.

In relationships of any kind, this implies elaborating on the major pain points. For example, if, for any number of reasons, you happen to miss (monetary) reward an employee that was legitimately expecting the reward, you should clearly show (in your official apology) that you are aware of the potential consequences.

For example, "I sincerely apologize for bypassing you this time. I feel really bad about the entire situation because I'm aware that you were counting on that extra cash and that my mistake probably caused you certain financial problems. I will send your well-deserved money as soon as possible; you can count on that."

In this example, we see all three elements of the "efficient" apology.

Let's dissect it…

"I sincerely apologize for bypassing you this time. I feel really bad about the entire situation because I'm aware that you were counting on that extra cash…"

In this instance, you are clearly elaborating on your feelings. This is important because it will trigger a certain level of compassion thanks to mirror neurons. After all, nobody expects pure perfection from the leader. Mistakes happen.

"...my mistake probably caused you certain financial problems..."

Now you are openly acknowledging the negative impact of your mistake. The common error people do is to get defensive and try to explain why some mistakes happened. To the one affected by it, that kind of explanation doesn't mean anything. It feels more like some lame justification nobody believes.

Finally, we are coming to the most important part - reparation:

"...I will send your well-deserved money as soon as possible; you can count on that."

Assuming that you will deliver on your promise, this right here is what builds your respect among the team. Not only that you are sympathizing with the person you did wrong to while clearly acknowledging the underlying consequences of your mistake; you are also respecting that person high enough to fix the situation in the shortest time.

Let's move deeper into an apology

The Science of "Sorry"

There is, in fact, a scientific study on the most optimal (efficient) construct of an apology. In 2018, three scientists (Polin, Lount, & Lewicki, 2018) researched the most optimal structure of an apology. To do that, they provided students with the context of a mistake and then gave them the list of apologies. The students were tasked to rate the apologies.

They concluded that the more elements exist in the structure of an apology, the more effective that apology is in rebuilding the trust with higher efficiency in competence-based trust violations compared to integrity-based ones.

In summary, they have identified the most optimal six elements that received the highest ratings:

1. An expression of regret
2. An explanation of the circumstances
3. **An admission of responsibility**
4. A clear proof of remorse
5. **A fix (solution)**
6. An absolution request

If it isn't possible to include all six elements, the focus should be placed on:

- An admission of responsibility
- A fix (solution)

These two carry the biggest weight in the entire structure. However, not even all (well-thought) six elements will help if an apology isn't communicated in person. We should never ignore the influence of handshakes, eye contact, body cues, and verbal communication.

But the real question is: as a manager, should you even apologize to an employee?

Observed from purely behavioral and biochemical perspectives, a leader should rarely (vocally or contextually) apologize! Instead, the deeds should convey the message.

In one incident during the war in formal Yugoslavia in the first half of the 90s, a platoon leader made a terrible mistake during the retreat. Instead of following the standard procedure that demands that the communication line should never be broken, the circumstances forced the young sergeant to leave almost half of his men behind the enemy lines. Once those he managed to extract realized what happened, the silent protest began. The condemnation of his actions was obvious and public.

However, instead of coming up with excuses or apologies, the brave sergeant went back through the enemy lines and single-handedly extracted 13 completely surrounded men; some of them seriously wounded.

When they have returned, it was clear that the platoon leader has successfully regained the former respect without saying a single word. In other words, if you did wrong to an employee, instead of wasting time with words, fix what's broken with your deeds and do it immediately.

That begs a simple question: how should you handle your mistakes in the first place?

Handling your mistakes

How many times does a baby fall on the ground before taking those first insecure steps?

We can all learn from babies because a) they never give up, and b) they are actively learning from their mistakes – something we have all been doing not so long ago.

The process that ultimately enables a human baby to walk inde-pendently starts with the **awareness of the existence of a mistake.**

By acknowledging the mistake through (objective) retroactive analysis of the steps that led to it, the brain is adding the outcome to a separate memory block so that the next time, that outcome would become certain (transitioning from the *unknown* into the *known*).

Unfortunately, some managers are living in denial, persistently, and stubbornly rejecting the very thought that they have made a mistake. Such an institute of infallibility has a far-reaching negative impact on all dependent levels, especially in organizations where the efficacy of a successive instance closely depends on the accuracy and efficiency of the preceding instance.

In the next phase, the brain is **learning from the situation**. For example, a baby immediately realizes that grabbing a leaf of a fig tree isn't a viable solution because it cannot sustain the force that acts upon it. The outcome is now certain so the variables (steps and actions that originally led to such an outcome) are now known and will immediately be deemed counterproductive and impeded in the future attempt.

In organizations, managers should use every opportunity to **convey new knowledge to the teams**; thus, actively transforming a mistake into a valuable learning tool. By doing so, they are a) leveraging a mistake in progress, and b) preventing a scenario in which every team member must go through the process to eventually learn and apply the correct approach.

Once you achieve this level of self-consciousness and accountability and when you develop a habit of conveying your knowledge to your team(s), the new reality will make a significant positive influence on all areas of your professional environment.

But there's something else you should practice.

How sharing credit improves your career

Your most imminent goal is to create a high-trust environment. For that to happen and have any long-term positive effect, two different instances need to acknowledge your core values.

One instance is the team you're managing and leading. The other is the senior management which is constantly assessing the added value you are bringing to the organization.

What are the most prominent traits of a promising manager that has real potential?

Confidence, team playing, and leadership skills.

What is the most unlikely shortcut to a) demonstrate all three, and b) add to the trust establishment?

Sharing credits because everybody is aware that you, as a manager, would not achieve a defined goal if it weren't for the team that put the intellectual and physical efforts in constructing that new reality.

While it seems like a zero-sum game, it is a win-win situation after all, because sharing credits conveys the message of utmost confidence.

> *Insecure leaders that secretly doubt their skills and capabilities will take credit instead of acknowledging the team effort.*

The most valuable gain you could fathom as a manager comes exactly from sharing credits. The gesture will imprint in the minds of your team members because people's sense of belonging depends on them being publicly recognized. It is the reflection of the duality that we are living in. The acceptance and recognition of one's contribution from a person whom one considers superior elevate one's feeling of self-satisfaction. Since a sense of accomplishment and contribution is the crucial measure of fulfillment, our minds will never forget who acknowledges our effort and provides us with the gratifying feeling of being recognized.

Sharing credits with contributors is a simple and logical gesture that has a far-reaching impact.

EIGHT

Cultivate Diversity and Inclusion in the Workplace

Diversity alone is not enough to drive high engagement.

Diversity practices are associated with a trusting climate that, in turn, is positively related to employee engagement. Furthermore, the relationship between diversity practices and trust climate is moderated by inclusion (Downey, Van Der Werff, Thomas, & Plaut, 2015).

In other words, the **perception of inclusion is the key** because, while trust is a significant mediator between diversity and high engagement, the effect is further increased only by a positive influence of inclusion.

Inclusion, therefore, *solidifies* the bond between the two and *strengthens* the cumulative effect.

To be included means:

Having a voice

Making that voice count

However, the primary effect of diversity and, subsequently, inclusion on the overall performance and output on both team and organizational levels is only achieved through active implementation of the policies. That is, if they remain on a theoretical level, they have no effect.

The Mechanics of Diversity

Diversity, in the context of high-trust organizations, implies several interconnected classifications:

- Gender
- Race
- Socio-economic status
- Socio-economic and geographical background
- Ideological beliefs
- Sexual orientation
- Age
- Physical and mental abilities

On the most fundamental level, this mash of different personalities creates an idea pool that drives innovation, creativity, and, subsequently, progress.

In the search for tangible proof, we don't have to move further from the social evolution of the human species and nature's principal notion of diversity.

Once adopted, the culture of social exchange (sharing) between fundamentally different individuals rendered the existing behavioral paradigm obsolete; thus, enabling the formation of the diverse, thriving communities. In other words, human species switched from self-focus (the original behavioral attitude) to group-focus. We stopped being solitude and hedonistic creatures and moved to a social species which set the foundations of our modern society.

> *This sudden quantum leap was realized through the culture of diversity (and inclusion).*

However, if we are seeking for the most recent -- and related -- business cases for diversity, Juliet Bourke and Bernadette Dillon[1] suggest examination of Qantas, an Australian-based airline company and Apple Inc.

In 2013, Qantas hit the record low. After 98 years in the industry, the company reported a 2.8 billion loss (AUD) just to completely reverse the situation only four years later. In 2017, the company made 850 million in profit after collecting a streak of industry awards for excellence and safety - at the same time ranking as Australia's most trusted organization. (Qantas, 2017)

According to Alan Joyce, the company's CEO, such an impressive shift was predominantly conditioned by the newly instated culture of diversity, trust, and inclusion.

In the case of Apple Inc., diversity is threaded into the very fabric of the company's narrative and global strategy. They (Apple) "look beyond the usual measurements" because they have long learned that "different perspectives from the variety of ways of seeing things create a potent environment of creativity and initiative that gives birth to ideas and methodologies."

In 2018, 33% of all employees in Apple were women. Of the total number of employees, there were 23% Asian, 14% Hispanic, 9% Black, 3% multiracial, and 1% Native Americans, Native Hawaiians, and Pacific Islanders. Given the U.S. demographics breakdown for the same year, Apple's workforce reflects the racial structure while gender spread exceeds the trends in the tech industry where the male population is still a prevailing demographics.

However, in the recent two years, Apple pushed the diversity agenda even more. 53% of the new hires are from historically unrepresented groups in the tech industry. Furthermore, 45% of leaders under 30 are women. At the same time, that specific age group (under 30) is seeing the highest increase in the hiring trend (35% of the total number of employees are those younger than 30). Among them, 25% are Asians, 18% are Hispanic, 12% are Black, 5% multiracial. Therefore, there is an obvious upward trend in racial diversity.

But here's the interesting part: the new hiring of White employees dropped by 10% (from 50%). Apple is, therefore, continuously betting on diversity and the culture of maximum inclusion like no other company.

Results?

In 2005, Apple's net income was (in millions of US $) $1,328. Only 14 years later, in 2019, the company's net income has risen forty-fold to staggering $55,256, making Apple the third-largest company in the U.S. by revenue.

And Apple and Qantas are not probing a theory here.

Recursive (adverse) bias and discriminatory patterns

During a period of one second, our conscious mind can process up to 40 impressions compared to 11 million that our subconscious mind processes in that same timeframe. We can assess the distance between the two objects in a split second without too much thinking, or drive a car, or make a simple mathematical calculation, or orientate to the sound we hear, and even decide whether or not that sound poses a threat. It's all happening instantly with the minimum effort thanks to the part of our mind that never sleeps and that is capable of "seeing" even when our eyes are completely shut[2].

These "automated" responses are commonly known as *instinctive,* and we are relying on them to go through our days with added ease.

However, some of those "conclusions" and subsequent decisions are influenced by implicit (subconscious) biases we have been developing since our earliest age; prejudices that we are not even aware of, that may easily affect logic. For first-time managers and, consequently, their companies, this can have devastating consequences.

Gender bias

> *Strong gender bias confirms that the positive influence of diversity is (completely) inhibited if there is no inclusion.*

Roughly 50% of the global population are women. If we apply the paradigm of the gender-equal ability of job execution across the industries while knowing the innate potential of women in organizational tasks, it is then reasonable to conclude that the organizations deprived of female input have limited potential.

Companies and institutions that are employing a high percentage or even a majority of women but not utilizing their collective trust of brains in problem-solving and decision-making are effectively estranging that corpus. It is a negative-sum game because decisions are lacking input from a significant party directly or indirectly involved in a process.

By default, in such conditions, the total gains and losses are always less than zero. As the rule of thumb, the only way to reverse the situation and maintain the status quo, at the very least, is to take something from another party. However, the imposed (gender-biased) culture blocks that request, consequently preventing reaching the equilibrium; thus, keeping the conditions in a perpetual negative balance.

The fact that those conditions are not triggering serious competition -- a natural occurrence of the negative-sum game, -- only proves the backwardness of the entire concept.

> *One of the best indicators that your organization is influenced by this bias is a prevailing perception of a proactive female employee that takes the initiative as aggressive while perceiving a male worker that exhibits a similar attitude as confident.*

According to a 2012 report on gender diversity and corporate performance by Credit Suisse Research Institute, "companies with at least one woman on the board have outperformed their peer group with no women on the board by 26% over the last six years." (Credit Suisse Research Institute, 2012)

Another significant finding of the research is that a woman in the board brings 4% higher return of equity and the same increase in the net income growth: 16% overall ROE compared to 12% of the companies without women in their boards; 14% NIG vs. 10% of those without at least one woman in the board.

Morgan Stanley's quantitative framework based on the comparative analysis of 1600 stocks globally, clearly shows that the companies with women in boards are delivering higher returns with less volatility, constantly outperforming companies run by homogeneous (men-only) boards. In the context of corporate settings, higher gender diversity (and inclusion) translates to increased productivity, greater innovation, improved decision-making, higher employee retention, and satisfaction. (Parker, et al., 2016)

There is a prevailing argument in favor of the broad inclusion of women in decision-making, yet they are making less than 25% in the management corpus globally.

Racial bias

No-dreadlocks business policy. One of the prime examples of racial biases and, at the same time, the most controversial subject with courts and government's institutions taking both sides of the argument. And the 2010 case of Chasity Jones best describes the consequences of such bias.

Jones was first offered a position in Catastrophe Management Solutions (CMS), an insurance company from Mobile, AL, just to be denied the job after she declined to cut her dreaded hair. HR manager approached Jones to inform her that the company does not allow dreadlocks and that she has to remove them if she wants the position. Three years later, the Equal Employment Opportunity Commission filed a lawsuit against CMS but has ultimately lost the case.

And even though projections show that by the year 2032, people of color will become the majority in the U.S. working class (Wilson, 2016), racial prejudice remains the factor that affects organizational diversity by denying active inclusion on all levels, particularly on the managerial functions. This discrepancy is best witnessed in 2018 Deloitte's report on minority representation in boards of Fortune 100 and 500 companies. Minorities make only 16.1% (912 seats) of the entire executive corpus.

Similarity bias

In October 2019, a Delaware-based, middle-sized accounting company announced a new series of hiring. During the two-week deadline, 334 candidates applied to 12 open positions.

Taught by previous negative experiences, the company's CEO requested all facial images, names, and gender specifics to be omitted from the CVs before the selection process. It's a well-thought practice that can, at least to some extent, result in a diversity of the employees' body. But it's not a guarantee!

Two HR managers, one man and one woman, then handpicked about half of the received candidacies for the next round where they will put applicants to various tests.

However, when additionally analyzed, it turned out that 73% of all selected applicants went to the same two universities the two HR managers graduated from.

Without a name or face or gender specifications, their brains have automatically started searching for anything even remotely associative that will help make the decision using minimum efforts. In other words, their decisions were under a predominant influence of the so-called, *similarity bias*. For example, tech companies in Silicon Valley are more likely to hire employees from UC Berkeley (Staley, 2017).

This particular (implicit) bias has a strong role in our existence because we are instinctively drawn to people similar to us due to the (aforementioned) innate duality of a modern human species. As such, its influence on our decision-making process should not be ignored.

Halo vs. Horns effect

It takes less than two seconds to form an opinion of a person, thing, or situation. And if that is a positive impression, we tend to expand on that profile by assigning the same positive attribute to every area of that person's life. For example, if we find someone attractive, we are most likely to think that the person is also intelligent and/or charismatic.

> *Therefore, a photo on a candidate's CV can be a determining factor in our decision to invite the candidate to an interview.*

Under the influence of this same bias, a manager can create a (false) positive image of an employee who did a good job on some project a couple of months ago (halo effect) or, on the other hand, make a diametrically opposite opinion of a worker who just failed once in a defined previous period (horns effect).

However, neither of these two situations confirms such a conclusion. Logic implies that the "A+" worker can fail at any given task and exhibit a downward trend in the overall performance while, at the same time, the "bad" one can radically improve, thus, effectively contradicting the constructed reality.

Nevertheless, this is one of those implicit biases that commonly affect a manager's rational thinking. Moreover, it also has a direct connection to another concept called *confirmation bias*.

Confirmation bias

Once we form an opinion, we tend to reject anything that confronts it and focus only on the information that directly and/or indirectly confirm it. This often leads to wrong assessments because we are subconsciously overlooking (ignoring) any opposing argument.

> *Awareness of confirmation bias is forcing companies to outsource critical analyses and estimations to the third-party providers.*

Combined with the halo effect, it can lead to a completely wrong decision and subsequently jeopardize the company's position in the market. This is best witnessed in brokerage companies and individual retail investors. Opposing signals are completely ignored which is causing a trader to execute an unfavorable trade order. However, it's not rare for managers of all levels, across the industries, to completely disregard even clear indicators that their decision has no ground in fundamental business logic.

Language (and accent) bias

Connected to halo effect and imposed (local) societal standards, language – and accent – bias can cause a manager to misjudge a candidate or an employee simply because we value phonetically "accurate" language and similar accents (similarity bias).

As Wilkinson suggested back in 1965, we (subconsciously) differentiate three different levels of accent "prestige:"

1. Standard
2. Urban
3. Rural

Our impression of a person will be largely influenced by how we identify the accent level. Halo and horn effects will do the rest and potentially cause a completely wrong assessment of a person's potential and the character itself.

ALL OF THESE BIASES HAVE A SERIOUS ADVERSE EFFECT ON BOTH the physical and mental health of those who feel in any way discriminated against. Consequently, their state directly affects the organization.

Adverse effects of discrimination

The anticipation of prejudice is enough to endanger health. (Sawyer, Major, Casad, Townsend, & Berry Mendes, 2012) The event immediately puts the body in psychological and cardiovascular stress as a response to a hostile environment. In other words, a person who anticipates some kind of discrimination exhibits an increased sympathetic response also knows as, *fight or flight response.*

The human body has only one way to defend from an unsafe environmental condition and that's immediate activation of the self-defense mechanism. Unfortunately, this doesn't come without consequences. Once initiated, the self-preservation mechanism inhibits several secondary mechanisms such as hair and nail growth, cellular regeneration, immune system activation, and - working memory. (Kuhlmann, Piel, & Wolf, 2005) (American Psychological Association)

In other words, a person with an elevated sympathetic response has an impaired (or completely disabled) capacities of rational thinking because the massive endocrine activation associated with the self-defense mechanism in humans and other mammals interferes with the ability to encode memory, effectively preventing the retrieval of information.

Therefore, as managers, we ought to ask ourselves two questions:

1. Can a person in that state make rational decisions?
2. How such decisions affect our processes?

Managing biases in a professional environment

To fight the bad, unleash the good

There are two goals to consider: (Vanderbilt, n.d.)

Fostering a culture of respect and inclusion.

This builds a high-trust organization which, in turn, ensures that your employees don't operate in a state of distress. Such organizations report a 50% higher output. (Roderick, 2009)

Two identifying factors of a high-trust professional environment are:

- Sense of belonging
- Mutual respect

The foundation of such an organization (the primary agenda) is *trust establishment*. That is to say, every effort has been made to eliminate, for instance, racial bias to completely remove the stress factor caused by the anticipation of any kind of dominant bias.

Once the paradigm has been successfully changed, employees feel safe, and that state of homeostasis then allows an employee to start identifying with the group. It is a built-in urge stemming from our survival instinct and inherited duality that is forcing us to connect with like-minded people. This tendency, however, is inhibited for as long as we are distressed in an environment, hence, operating in a self-preservation mode.

Equity and Inclusion

The policy of exclusion forms a culture of single-mindedness. These types of organizations are inherently limited in their ability to understand the conditions outside their constructed reality.

This, consequently, deprives such organizations of freshness and new vitality (i.e. expanded idea pool, positive energy common for newcomers, etc.) that come with differences. At the same time, the culture of single-mindedness commonly inhibits equity, and that fact renders the sole notion of a high-trust organization impossible.

Therefore, by creating an open-minded culture, a manager is automatically implementing the equity notion that leads to inclusion and closes the loop that builds a high-trust organization. Inclusion then begins harnessing the immense (previously locked) potential of diversity.

Benefits of non-biased professional environments

Diversity, a basic principle of the world around us, builds an environment that leverages creativity and high levels of innovation that emerge as the result of improved relationships.

These factors are essential in community-building processes that ultimately deliver increased productivity. The organization built on these principles takes a tribe-like form.

However, the success of this implementation depends on the ability of the management of all levels to root out biases. But that mitigation process has to start on an individual (personal) level.

Reducing implicit biases in the personal lives of employees (and managers equally) as the essential first step

Through specialized (theme) workshops, managers should incentivize their team members to take the essential first step: **identifying self-developed biases through self-analysis**.

The paradigm here is simple: to solve the problem, one first has to acknowledge the existence of the problem.

In the next stage, we analyze our closest social environment.

As a social species, we are pre-programmed to adjust to our physical and social environment. One of the prerequisites of the adaptation process is the adoption of prevailing moral and societal standards of the group.

Such exposure inevitably creates a set of prejudices because every community makes its common global *acceptance and rejection policies*. In other words, every member of the group is pre-programmed to automatically accept or reject someone's expression based on the set of inherited protocols.

These protocols are then "imported" to every new environment unless there is a strong policy that challenges those principles in which case, a person is either accepting the new set of rules and slowly changing the original paradigm or abandoning the environment altogether.

The role of a manager in this process is to motivate each individual to a) reflect on the original (inherited) prejudices and then b) create a necessary cognitive distance. This goal is best achieved through open discussions.

These discussions on the group level open the exchange process through which members are **a) sharing their experiences and b) actively absorbing those coming from others.**

The single best proof of the efficiency of this particular approach is the Alcoholics Anonymous organization. Members help each other through the continuous sharing of individual experiences. Mentors are actively motivating new members to share their stories. This kind of communication has a positive impact on the alteration of the *loop of habit* where we are changing a bad habit with the good one that ultimately spreads to other areas of our lives. (Duhigg, 2012)

And since the process of the elimination of biases is effectively a process of habit alteration, a manager should, therefore, **entice open-mindedness to create and foster a culture that inhibits stereotypes and over-generalization**. (Both of these are common traits of narrow-minded people.)

However, for this to return the desired results, employees must be held accountable, and, most importantly, emotions must be separated from facts. In other words, a person must "override" the influence of the subconscious mind and emotions.

This is done through the elemental process of central belief system alteration, where the right cerebral hemisphere is provided with a critical amount of information that contradicts the original belief system locked inside the left cerebral hemisphere. (Athene, 2015)

When this occurs, the right hemisphere successfully challenges the left and starts breaking down the constructed reality[3]. On the most fundamental level, the existing memory blocks and corresponding decision-making protocols are then compared to the newly imported information to ultimately decide which principles provide better survival odds.

For example, in a criminal investigation, after a suspect's energy reserves have been deflated due to mental exhaustion, the "instinctive" response is to accept the offered deal since our brains are programmed to avoid extensive mental efforts and uncomfortable conditions.

Therefore, to separate emotions and the influence of the subconscious mind from cognitive intent to ultimately suppress the influence of bias, one must stop separating information on acceptable and unacceptable and, instead, absorb every piece of information without discrimination as the only way to break through the previously constructed reality and live open-mindedly. This is an example of a personal goal of every team member, and a manager should closely monitor the progress.

Only now can we harness the true purpose of the dual-hemisphere brain and effectively "lock the deal".

As we now know, two brain hemispheres play a predominant role in the process of *mastering skills*. Continuous practice with incremental complexity of the tasks is building up neuronal connections between the two hemispheres. With every new connection, we are becoming better at a given skill.

It is argued that each of us is capable of mastering any skill with brute dedication and adequate practice.

It is, therefore, reasonable to conclude that the perpetual education in implicit and explicit biases and their negative impact on the progress of our society should eventually result in perfect understanding and a complete change of paradigms.

Mitigating the risks associated with a bias-driven culture in a professional environment

As we have already explained, personal biases are unconsciously imported into a professional environment where they commonly influence the decision-making process. For first-time managers, one of the agendas in building a high-trust organization is to identify rooted organizational biases (i.e. similarity bias, confirmation bias, gender discrimination, halo effect, etc.)

This is essential in determining the areas and processes affected by those biases.

For example, an obvious low level of diversity commonly implies the predominant influence of an array of prejudices in the hiring process. In the first instance, a manager can easily interrupt a negative practice through active involvement and implementation of the new protocols:

- "Blind" interviews (requires an adjusted ad copy) instead of the classic ones so that hiring staff cannot be influenced by biases.

In practice, this implies a resume without a candidate's name, photo, gender details, race, height, and the name of the educational institution(s) a candidate graduated from. An additional practice of conducting true blind interviews (preventing visual contact) has proved itself as the best way to create diversity in the professional environment.

- An extra layer of control over the hiring process to ensure that the newly instated policy is in effect.
- The interview questions should focus on the required skills rather than on superficial data. For instance, presenting a candidate with a real problem he or she will inevitably encounter and assess the level of expertise immediately after the candidate provides a detailed solution(s). (Williams & Mihaylo, 2019)

The purpose of such an approach is to ensure a diverse environment in which a manager can reap the benefits of different ideas and perspectives. If we know that each of us has been influenced by the own set of circumstances such as origin, individual experiences, and the way we perceive them, type and place of education, etc., we can then conclude that our opinions differ even when on the same track. Those deviations are what lead to unlikely solutions.

Assuming that we have successfully reduced the adverse effects of biases within the organization (or that we are actively working on that mission), our next agenda is to create an environment of unchallenged inclusion.

Building the culture of inclusion

In the most basic sense, inclusion means that EVERY employee, regardless of the "rank" and overall responsibilities, must have a voice. In other words, an employee, by default, has a "seat at the roundtable" and "opinion" in discussions.

The common problem managers encounter in the early stage of their new appointment is the tendency (and rooted culture) of the male employees to ignore the inputs of the female employees and/or to take the credit for their solutions. In another instance, veteran team members are notorious for their suppressive attitude toward new employees.

Each of these example situations contradicts the basic notion of inclusion and should, therefore, be eliminated.

The question is how to achieve a consensual disengagement of such negative practices.

We can start by applying a simple military practice.

In training routines involving physical fitness, soldiers take turns as designated "trainers." This seemingly simple "responsibility" ensures that every soldier experiences leadership in the early stage. At the same time, such practice creates an environment of inclusion which is a prerequisite for building a high-trust organization – a fundamental request for a successful military unit and/or installation.

In civil affairs, particularly in business organizations, the same effect can be achieved by rotating team members in leadership roles in the meetings. This includes all employees regardless of the level of their contribution. Such practice allows a manager a simple insight into the possibly suppressed or hidden potential of a team member that otherwise lacks the initiative.

On the more general (household) level, managers should organize the rotation of the employees on running the underlying office errands and chores (logistics). Again, this is nothing more than applying yet another proven military practice where each trainee goes through every segment of combat training, logistic preparations, and maintenance.

The logic behind such a model of management is founded in the group's built-in tendency to reach the majority decision on the new leader after assessing the individual potentials in a wide array of regular and extraordinary social situations.

Again, the request for accountability must be fulfilled for any of this to yield desired results. At the same time, managers are obligated to react on any disruptive attempt aimed against the normal unfolding of the community-building processes. That predominantly implies a timely response to a bias-driven and selfish type of behavior.

---

1. Bourke, J., & Dillon, B. (2018). *The diversity and inclusion revolution: eight powerful truths*. Deloitte Review.
2. 2013 research done by Burra et al proves that our brain can "see" even if we are completely blind. Scientists exposed a patient with complete cortical blindness to block of faces. Some depictions showed gazes directed toward

the patient while others away from him. fMRI scan showed "increased right amygdala activation in response to directed compared with an averted gaze" in the region associated with the larger network that handles face and gaze processing.

3. For as long as our beliefs are unchallenged, our central belief system is stable. Even the brain will help by sending hormone *norepinephrine* to prevent entrance and nesting of any information that is contradictory to an already established set of principles. However, if we suddenly change our environment (i.e. moving from a traditional rural to a high-end urban area, being arrested for committing a felony, etc.), our central belief system needs to undergo certain adjustments to survive in this new environment. (Athene, 2015)

NINE

Use Challenging Conversation as a Tool to Strengthen Relationship

Before entering tough conversations, managers should contemplate on two goals:

1. *At the end of the discussion, we have actionable steps to resolve the issue*
2. *We can maintain a good relationship with the employee after addressing the problem*

It is in our nature to avoid uncomfortable situations because the sole anticipation puts the body in a state of acute distress. However, one of the realities of every manager is a situation where we need to deliver negative feedback, address some issues, or execute corrective actions on the teams. These instances are inevitably causing inhibition of serotonin activation on an individual or group level (depending on the situation). The consequences are acute depression and recuperation time.

For many managers, especially those that are newly appointed and have no experience, this is one of the most challenging aspects of the role and has proven itself as a potential deal-breaker or the factor that can impair the overall effort in building a high-trust organization.

What many are not realizing is that it is possible to build trust even with challenging conversations.

Utilizing tough conversations in the trust-building process

The most important request is to **change the common paradigm of *telling* into a *dialogue***, meaning that, instead of simply communicating the issue (one-sided), a manager should entice conversation.

This, in turn, re-establishes the trust base previously built on the policy of inclusion. In other words, an employee feels less distressed due to the given opportunity to participate in problem-solving.

For example, an error on the specific part of the project is essentially a problem. Simply reprimanding a team member responsible for the error is effectively canceling the notion of inclusion; thus, affecting the trust base. However, if a manager initiates a discussion on the issue, the error transforms into a learning tool for the entire group. In such circumstances, a team member doesn't suffer any serious serotonin inhibition which, in turn, reduces the recuperation time.

This approach requires planning. That is to say, a manager should have at least a basic idea of what to say, how to say it, and what areas to cover for the discussion to yield a positive result and, subsequently, optimal feedback.

However, there's a threat, hiding in such a request.

The response should always be timely. Addressing an issue that is far in the past is pointless in most cases (the statute of limitations came into effect). On the other hand, reacting too soon while still in an agitated state due to the anticipation and/or realization of the consequences means that the response will be heavily influenced by emotions.

This contradicts the next two requests and that's calmness and rational thinking.

It is physiologically impossible to satisfy these requests while experiencing an increased sympathetic response.

Hence, in weighing between these two options (timely response vs. homeostatic initial state), the latter bears higher significance. Therefore, before engaging an employee or a team in a negative context, a manager should allow the necessary recuperation time to reduce the influence of emotions.

During the conversation or at the end of it, depending on the complexity of the issue at hand, it is necessary to set rational expectations. These are, effectively, the goals assigned to an individual employee or team in general. The assignees are held responsible for achieving those goals for the corrective measure to have the expected effect.

Now, there are "studies" that suggest picking a neutral ground because calling an employee into the office shifts the power balance. What is presumably ignored in these kinds of claims is the fact that we are leaders and that we must be perceived as such. The role of a manager does not contradict the notions of diversity, inclusion, and high-trust organizations. In fact, it is required and necessary because teams cannot function without leadership. At the same time, team members have to have at least a minimum level of respect so by calling an employee into your office, you are maintaining the proper balance of power.

As long as you are ensuring that the discussion is collaborative, there will be no adverse effects on the trust base.

The analogy is a football team in the practice session. The trainer will closely monitor individual and team performance and will stop the session the moment he notices a mistake. Depending on the situation, the trainer will either take a player on the side and calmly explain the error while setting the expectation or use the opportunity for a group lesson. In both instances, the player(s) has a say and can even challenge the corrective measure. This opens the discussion and commonly leads to a better solution.

But the main point is to be in a position to notice an error and a manager can only do that if being actively involved in the processes just like the football trainer is. The next request is a timely address with the basic plan to fix the mistake which then evolves into a much complex and more effective solution thanks to the multiple inputs. Hence, reaping the benefits of an inclusive environment.

But everything so far begs a simple question:

How to handle tough conversations?

Among the top ten most difficult conversations, the first four occur in the workplace: (Scott, 2015)

1. Asking for a raise (and denying it)
2. Colleagues' inappropriate behavior
3. Feedback on poor performance (at both sender and receiver)
4. Asking for a promotion (and denying it)

It might sound illogical to list these life-essentials as the most difficult topics but in the core of that discomfort lies the fear of rejection. The higher the stakes, the stronger the fear. The stronger the fear, the more devastating the consequences. The raise is a high-stake game and as such, triggers the highest level of stress. Even the anticipation (the thought) is enough to put the body in distress since it is the matter of survival.

While it is challenging for both parties, managers, by default, are expected to handle these conversations in a way that doesn't affect the underlying trust base of the organization (team, group, company).

There are two principal approaches to mitigate the risks: (Knight, 2015)

1. In the first instance, a manager should be clear, concise, direct, and unemotional
2. In the second, however, the entire process should be broken into phases and accompanied by empathy

The optimal approach depends on the circumstances. For example, if you are delaying the decision to lay off a particular employee simply because you feel uncomfortable even after all conditions for such a decision have been met and after exhausting every available option to prevent that outcome (i.e. additional training, repressive measures, etc.), you would ideally choose the first option because lingering any longer just increases potential consequences for the organization.

On the other hand, if the situation isn't caused by an employee either directly or indirectly (i.e. strategical cuts), you should opt in for the second approach where you'll openly discuss the new circumstances with the employee. The reason why you would want to use this particular approach in the given situation is that you might end up with an unlikely solution that is beneficial for both parties (i.e. willingness of the employee to accept an alternative position within the organization). This doesn't necessarily have to happen during the initial conversation and that's the reason why you should break it into a few meetings to let the employee absorb the situation and reach a cognitive decision after being provided with the available alternatives.

4-Step protocol

Judy Ringer, a conflict and communication skills trainer, suggests four steps in handling difficult conversations that can be applied to the working environment and management in particular. In such a context, the protocol can be best utilized in resolving issues that are formed during the project management process.

The first step is an INQUIRY. The notion implies that, as a manager, you exhibit a certain level of curiosity by letting an employee present the situation and possibly explain the underlying causes that have led to a mistake.

In the next step, a manager ACKNOWLEDGES the argument (whether or not that argument has been deemed agreeable). In other words, you find bits and pieces on which you can agree with an employee to ease the tensions. Your acknowledgment sends a message that you were actively listening and have ultimately accepted the provided explanation. This step is justified through the notion of inclusion.

Step three: ADVOCACY or the stage where you are delivering your point of view but without diminishing, ignoring or rejecting the arguments of the opposing party. This is the essential factor of any effective conversation because it implies open-mindedness rather than an authoritarian standpoint.

Finally, in the final step, both parties engage in PROBLEM-SOLVING. The critical thing here is for each party to find something acceptable in the opposing party's argument and build on that. Avoiding or ignoring this request cancels the fundamental intention of this protocol and that's finding a mutually satisfying solution or, at the very least, limiting the consequence.

Example Scenarios

To bring this subject even closer, we will go over some of the common situations that inevitably trigger tough conversations.

Addressing poor performance (Conley, 2019)

The first thing a manager should do before engaging an employee with this particular (and common) issue is to assess all the factors that could potentially lead to poor performance that was outside the employee's control. It comes down to contemplating set goals, providing training resources, motivation factors, and employee's personal issues.

In the next stage, a manager explains the problem concisely by using tangible data derived from measurements on benchmarking and meta-comparison. There is no room for emotions here or casting premature judgments.

Now comes the opposing party's perceptive on the issue similar to the inquiry step in a previously explained protocol.

After acknowledging the employee's standpoint, the case and arguments should be summarized. Here, a manager identifies the points of disagreement while emphasizing the common grounds.

Finally, the process ends with brainstorming the solution. In most cases, this involves additional training or relocation of the employee to a more appropriate position considering the most prominent skills. However, in some instances, the entire situation can result in contract termination after it becomes clear that the employee is refusing to accept arguments, advice, or instructions.

Violation of dress and grooming policies (ADP, 2017)

According to the ADP's advice, this issue should unfold in four sequential yet interconnected steps.

In the opening step, a manager is **announcing the** upcoming **discussion** with an employee to raise awareness. It is not uncommon that employees are completely unaware of the problem.

Next, the manager should **consider applicable laws** to prevent problem escalation. For example, specific minority rights or rights associated with certain disabilities.

At the same time, every effort should be made to **prevent the assumption** of different causes such as health conditions that can result in poor hygiene or less-than-appropriate outfit.

Finally, set the expectation and document the entire case with precise remarks about solutions.

Inability to provide (expected) raises

When employees are accustomed to receiving regular annual pay raises, the sudden shift in paradigm can cause devastating consequences and completely cancel the established trust base and subsequent engagement and productivity.

To mitigate these risks, make sure that you announce the change in the policy early on.

In 2008, a small yacht-making company from Eastern Europe found itself in a dire situation after 70% of the orders were canceled in less than a month due to the crisis outbreak. In those circumstances, small and middle-sized manufacturers of luxury products are first to take the hit.

However, despite the situation, the company did not even consider lay-offs. Instead, the Board has decided to cut the operational costs to hedge against potential illiquidity. That strategy first and foremost implied freezing the paychecks on all levels.

The CEO broke the news to the employees three months before the usual pay raise period and made sure to carefully elaborate on all circumstances that have led to such a decision. It turned out that the employees were not even aware of a devastating chain of events that was taking place on the other side of the world, namely the bankruptcy of Lehman Brothers on September 15 that same year. None of them could even fathom the extent of such an event until the CEO explained it, step-by-step.

By the end of the meeting, nobody was even thinking about the fact that they have just been informed that no raise will happen that year.

Therefore, by providing a wide context of the circumstances and their causal relationship, managers can prevent a mass dissatisfaction and even a wide-scale mutiny. In the high-trust organization, employees are closely connected and have uncon-ditional faith in their leadership. Together, they can go through some of the most difficult circumstances just to emerge stronger in the aftermath.

That's the underlying power of the organization based on diversity with the strong inclusion policy.

However, not even such a tight-knitted group is completely immune to sudden changes; especially if they imply new management. As a new executive, you are inheriting a system that is on standby. The structure is established, habits are deeply rooted, but disappointment far exceeds expectations. In other words, your new team is wary because the trust has been broken.

The question is, how do you fix it?

TEN

Rebuilding Broken Trust

For new managers, there are two instances early on where it is necessary to initiate a trust rebuilding process. The first one occurs immediately after taking a new role.

I f you make a promise to your team and fail to deliver on that promise, would confession and an apology affect your leadership? Could it be perceived as a sign of weakness?

New managers tend to get carried away while giving their first speeches. This mostly implies making immediate promises that are rooted in over-optimistic expectations that have no real ground in the organization they are taking over. And your new team is aware of those limits.

Those experienced never make that mistake for three simple reasons:

- First impressions count the most

- Early breach of trust cannot be reversed that easily as opposed to the breach in an already established trustful relationship (Ohio State University, 2009)
- The new team's default state is wariness

Therefore, a **negative first impression would have a devastating impact on a future relationship**.

This feature is directly connected to our self-preservation mechanism through which we are assessing the conditions in our immediate environment. In some instances, it takes less than two seconds to assess a person or situation and build that first (negative or positive) impression.

It is a necessary first step in our threat evaluation process that allows us to ultimately decide whether the environment is safe or not. Meeting a new person, in private or professional life equally, inevitably triggers this self-defense mechanism and re-initiates the trust-building process. Hence, the team's state of wariness and mistrust.

Reversing a default state

In an event where a new manager has been installed, the team is automatically labeling the manager as the *unknown known*; thus, resetting the trust-building process.

This is causing a decrease in an overall level of trust on the organizational level since the team is on standby, awaiting the first set of mistakes and/or successes to change the label in one out of two possible ways:

1. Discredited; hence, not to be trusted
2. Accredited (successful, confident); therefore, trustworthy

Here's the major pain point for new managers and a hard trap to avoid: **breaching trust early on inhibits the trust-building process.**

In other words, failing to deliver on a promise BEFORE you have established a trust base with your new team means that you will be having difficulties reversing the consequences. And making early promises is inevitable because it is expected.

The analogy is an early onset of a potentially romantic relationship since the same mechanisms control the trust-building process in both instances. In such a situation, the potential for a long-term trustful relationship is canceled by the early breach of trust (i.e. adultery or unauthorized conveying of shared sensitive information to a third party).

Since the first condition of forming (or joining) a group (especially the elemental one) is trust, due to our pre-programmed duality, the "betrayal" equals rejection. By default, the rejection event immediately inhibits *serotonin* and, subsequently, *oxytocin* activation, consequently breaking the still weak (emotional) connection.

As time goes by and the emotional connection strengthens, the stakes are proportionally rising, making it difficult for either party to break the relationship regardless of the severity of the underlying cause. For example, a long-term emotional relationship has a high odd of surviving even the ultimate betrayal such as infidelity.

Therefore, the logic implies that the new manager should refrain from making unobjective promises early on.

The simplest trick to maintain the self-control is to apply a defense lawyers' paradigm of *"never asking a question to which you don't already know the answer."* In other words, the "promise" should not exit the realm of what is absolutely possible considering all the circumstances (i.e. the new and relatively unknown environment, level of experience, unfamiliarity with root habits, and practices within the organization, etc.).

Hence, arguably the best strategy to reverse the default state and successfully initiate the trust-building process so you could reap the benefits of the high-trust organization is to put everything you have learned thus far in practice first and start making promises second. That is to say, make a promise to a team that trusts you and/or start with "light" and achievable promises.

WITH THIS BEING THE FIRST (IMMEDIATE) INSTANCE IN WHICH A new manager is forced to actively engage in a trust-building process, the second one is definitely the first failed delivery on the promise. It can be a raise, reaching a certain goal, or anything else that can be felt like a betrayal.

Counteracting the negative effect of betrayal and reversing the situation

Making promises (assuring your team members into something) is given and inevitable due to the underlying nature of the managerial role. Leaders are pushing teams forward by inspiring them and that implies promising certain successes. Unfortunately, more often than not, a "promised" success turns into a failure and disappointment.

Since the perceived social hierarchy plays a crucial role in our emotional responses in interpersonal conduct, the consequence is amplified due to the built-in class disparity between a leader and team members. In other words, in equal circumstances, we will experience a significantly lower intensity of the negative emotional response if our co-worker fails to deliver on a promise than we would feel if a leader makes the same mistake.

The good analogy is the 2008/09 global financial crisis where we felt betrayed by those, we placed on the leadership roles. Bankers and hedge funds executives quickly became globally despised and labeled as the enemies of the people. Just a few months earlier, people were admiring them for their almost unnatural ability to drive economic growth.

Therefore, **the higher is a leader's status, the greater is the class disparity, and thus, the stronger is the consequence of the leader's failure.** Even the most insignificant errors can feel like a deep emotional betrayal.

How do you ensure that you keep the promises (in the realm of possibility) to avoid the potential trust breach?

Begin by focusing on the quality rather than quantity of your commitments.

In other words, identify (understand) the (at-hand) primary request or demand. For example, better working conditions in a sense of more open discussions, respect, inclusiveness, or improvements in a physical environment.

Pick the one you can definitely deliver with the least risk or investment and commit to it.

In any organization, there's a valuable "freebie" that doesn't require anything more than a leader's dedication. For instance, push forward the agenda of immediate inclusiveness and deliver on the promise immediately. Organize a meeting and make it clear to everyone that you are interested in everyone's opinions equally.

An all-applicable metaphor is a high-ticket affiliate product salesmanship.

The trick of this profitable game isn't to *promise the best deal* but merely to **show that you care.** Remember what Roosevelt said, "People don't care how much you know until they know how much you care."

First of all, it is questionable whether or not you can actually offer a reasonable discount or upsell. Second of all, even if you could do it, that would mean depriving yourself of a profit.

To bypass this entanglement, a seller is focusing on a few principal benefits a prospect would be able to reap after purchasing the product. Neither of these benefits is stemming from the seller's personal investment. They are what the circumstances allow.

For example, let's say that you are selling a $2,000 vacuum cleaner. Your market is virtually any household in the world with a dusty surface. However, every such household already owns a $100 vacuum cleaner that is perfectly capable of dealing with that issue. Then again, they would all like to own the expensive version but the price tag is definitely a deterring factor.

Therefore, the dust issue won't cut it anymore. The problem isn't potent enough. Hence, the escalation. The product quickly evolves from just another shiny vacuum cleaner into a complete health solution capable of preventing some of the worst respiratory diseases that could lead to death. The narrative needs to deliver a vivid image of a situation so that every time a new owner uses the product, he or she feels immediate relief. In this case, dealing with microscopic nemeses that threaten the lives of every family member.

So now **the benefit justifies the investment**.

A $2,000 vacuum cleaner is what you are expecting from the team and that expectation is stemming from the demands placed in front of you by the senior executive staff. That's why they hired or promoted you in the first place.

However, your team, given the current conditions, can only deliver and it is, therefore, interested, in a $100 device. The price is simply too much to pay when you consider the circumstances (the hourly wage, working conditions, company's attitude towards employees, etc.)

How do you sell them the more expensive version without compromising yourself? How do you deliver what's expected from you without incurring additional costs to the company? How do you ask them to invest more than they are willing to invest?

You can't simply offer a discount because the *discount* in our context would mean lowering the imposed expectations (which is not an option), or offering a raise or some kind of a one-time monetary reward (again, not an option).

But if you commit yourself to work alongside them on a joint goal…?

What's the universal issue employees have with their jobs?

They don't like their boss. They despise the very notion of it. Yet, they all yearn for the boss' recognition and praise.

It's a certain paradox that only shows the class disparity between the two groups. Like patricians and plebeians of the Roman Empire. Both exist and both are vital for the functioning of the empire but one group holds greater rights than the other. However, if you bridge the gap and get closer; then you'll reap an unlikely benefit of raving support because your *divine* "descent" among the *mortals* is perceived as an act of recognition of their values.

In other words, your presence alone will kick-start the built-in competitiveness at each member. The cumulative effect will be increased productivity.

And all you've promised was to bleed alongside with them. A single promise of an unlikely benefit with a far-reaching impact that effectively sells a $2,000 vacuum cleaner.

It is relatively easy to identify the need you can satisfy so that you could make a necessary and largely expected promise and ultimately deliver upon it. It's the game every manager in the world is playing daily. You just have to study the situation and pick your battles.

But what about the promises made by your predecessor? Is your installment rendering them obsolete?

Inherited commitments

A promise made means a destination defined.

As a rule of thumb, organizations survive the changes in the executive staff because they have developed habits. In other words, the event doesn't cause processes to halt or cease. They can, however, slow down. Certain well-architected goals that are on their way to be achieved can accidentally end up disregarded or de-ranked on the list.

One of the reasons for this to happen is the aforementioned state of wariness, especially among those chosen by your predecessor to carry out certain assignments. When they hear that someone else is taking over, they become uncertain about the previously set goal(s). This status quo occurs because the originally formed bond has been broken which is, consequently, blocking the path to the chosen destination.

In the original agreement, a manager's role was to keep the team on the right path. With that person gone, the path is now unclear and, thus, the process is put on hold.

The only way for you to understand not only the circumstances but the sole existence of the promise and, therefore, the goal, is to ask, plain and simple.

However, asking alone is not enough because a simple answer is not always enough to grasp the essence of the problem they were trying to solve. Additionally, the new situational development (losing the leader and getting a substitute that has yet to be approved) can result in emotional outbreaks that commonly cloud the judgment and affect the elaboration of the problem.

And that leads us to arguably **the most effective strategy** you are about to use every time there is a need to rebuild broken trust.

The Power of ACTIVE LISTENING

Every time someone breaks trust, he or she is effectively creating a conflict. The only way to solve the conflict is to engage in negotiations. And arguably the best source to look for guidance when it comes to successful crisis resolution is the Federal Bureau of Investigation's Crisis Negotiation Unit (FBI CNU).

CNU is known for using eight techniques in every negotiation process: (Thompson, 2013)

1) EMOTION LABELLING or the effort of a negotiator to acknowledge the current state of mind of an opposing party.

By validating the person's emotions, you are effectively restoring the balance since you are taking the emotional response into the equation; thus, better understanding the underlying causes of dissatisfaction.

2) PARAPHRASING or repeating the person's statements in a much shorter form but in your own words while making every effort to avoid any minimalization of the person's experiences and/or emotional consequence(s).

3) MIRRORING or repeating the last 3 to 4 words the person said at the end of a single session.

By doing so, you are validating the statement, subsequently building rapport with the person.

The reason why this simple technique is successful is that it aims at the core of everyone's primary interests and that's to be heard, acknowledged, and recognized. Repeating the last few words sends a clear signal that you are actively listening which serves as the confirmation of the aforementioned core interests of every human being.

4) DYNAMIC INACTIVITY or making deliberate pauses before taking a turn in ongoing verbal communication.

The silence acts as a calming agent which is essential in every conflict resolution process since the primary demand is to achieve the transition from emotional to cognitive responding as quickly as possible.

Additionally, the pause enables the person you are communicating with to continue or end the thought. In other words, by making deliberate pauses, you are preventing interruptions of the flow of thoughts which could be recognized as the sign of aggression.

5) "I" MESSAGES or the effort to counteract the non-conducive statements that are affecting collaboration.

This particular technique partially relies on the so-called, "power of because" paradigm since the construct of the sentence commonly includes the word *because* that offers an explanation and, by default, removes the *unknown* from the equation.

However, the true purpose is to send the message that the other party is not collaborating. It is, essentially, a short sentence that contains a clear expression of the emotional response you've experienced on account of a specific claim or the entire conversation. In other words, it is a reality check you can use to restore the path of the otherwise derailed conversation that obviously leads in an unwanted direction.

Note that the tone you are using and the choice of words should not, in any way, be understood as a sign of aggression or the nested argument.

6) OPEN-ENDED QUESTIONS or the attempt to extract additional information by enticing a person to provide a wider context.

7) MINIMAL ENCOURAGES or the verbal and non-verbal signals that motivate the person to continue speaking.

Nodding your head or saying "I see," acts enticing and subtly forces the person to proceed with further elaboration of the circumstances. The purpose is to gain a wider view of the situation to reach the best possible conclusion.

8) SUMMARIZING or contracting everything a person said in a short version.

This is the vital final step of every negotiation process because the person perceives the summary as the ultimate validation, subsequently feeling the immediate relief.

The purpose is two-fold. On one hand, you are buying a necessary time to come up with a reasonable argument or solution. The analogy is a student who is deliberately repeating the professor's question in an attempt to construct an answer from the partial information stored in memory blocks.

On the other hand, you are building rapport and trust since the summary acts as validation and thus, recognition. This, in turn, helps you to influence the person's original standpoints and ultimately entice the person to adopt a proposed alternative.

THE QUESTION IS WHY WOULD YOU WANT TO ENGAGE IN SUCH A complex process to resolve a conflict?

Because you are effectively rebuilding a broken trust and to finalize the process, the parties involved need to go through seven stages: (Reinna, Reinna, & Hudnut, 2017)

Acknowledgment:
(of the consequence)
↓
Emotional expression
(of everyone affected)
↓
Support
↓
Reframing the experience
(providing a wider context)
↓
Taking responsibility:
↓
Forgiving
(collective forgiveness)
↓

Moving on

THIS IS THE CORRECT PATH OF THE HEALING PROCESS THAT ultimately restores trust and it is required in a situation when a certain change causes a breach in trust.

You start by engaging in active listening to understand circumstances, individual standpoints, and emotional or material consequences in order to have a detailed overview of the conflicting situation.

Once you have all the necessary information, you can begin the aforementioned trust-restoring process by moving through all seven stages.

Afterword

The origin of every low-trust organization and/or relationship is the sum of the personal lives of everyone involved. Members are unwittingly importing their own sets of fears, resentments, potential narrow-mindedness, prejudices, habits, and distrust. If left unattended for any longer time, this environment of aggregated negativism and self-constraining behaviors will ultimately self-destruct - without exceptions and at any given moment.

In 1888, George Eastman founded Eastman Kodak Company. Later known just as Kodak, the company pioneered the consumer market for amateur photography and, at the same time, the technology that will ultimately allow filming of the Hollywood movies. Kodak products quickly found their way into almost every household on the planet.

By the end of the 60s of the last century, Eastman's company had the majority market share in the industry with over $4 billion in sales while employing staggering 100,000 people. Kodak's solutions were used in filming John Glenn orbiting the Earth in 1962. Even the very first image of the planet from space had been taken using Kodak systems.

Still, in 2012, Kodak filed for bankruptcy, and the seed of that dreadful outcome can be traced back to 1975 and a single decision caused by the narrow-mindedness and discontinuation of the inclusivity and diversification practices - the two features that made the company great in the first place.

In 1975, Steve Sasson, one of Kodak's engineers, approached the Board with an unlikely innovation - a filmless photography device or **the world's first digital camera**.

"My prototype was big as a toaster, but the technical people loved it," Sasson said to the New York Times reporter on one occasion, "But it was filmless photography, so management's reaction was, 'that's cute - but don't tell anyone about it.'"

Almost two decades later, a former vice-president of Kodak, Don Strickland, will state, "We developed the world's first consumer digital camera, but we could not get approval to launch or sell because of fear of the effects on the film market." In 1993, Strickland will leave Kodak after several failed attempts to persuade the company to start manufacturing and marketing digital cameras.

The entire situation begs a simple question:

How did a company that can thank its success only to openness toward innovations, diversity, and inclusiveness come to the point where their leaders are afraid to even consider a change?

The leaders of Kodak in the 70s perceived digital photography as this disruptive technology that could threaten the company's dominant position. The burden of responsibility toward shareholders and investors who were only interested in profit discouraged them from entering the still uncharted territory.

Unfortunately, this over-cautious approach will quickly take roots and evolve so, in the 90s, the company's senior executive staff had an already developed organizational habit that caused them to narrowly focus on the success of the film and not see a rapidly developing situation in digital photography. Consequently, by the time when they finally decided to enter the race, it was already too late.

You see, regardless of how things appear on the first glance, you are, by default, entering the low-trust arena. And we've elaborated on the underlying reasons not so long ago.

Therefore, your first and foremost job is to reverse the paradigm, starting with the "handshake" that sends a clear message to everyone: "**I'm here to work with all of you so we would become the tip of the spear of this entire organization.**"

Does it sound like something nearly impossible to achieve?

What you've perhaps failed to realize is that you've just gone through a precise list of action steps with accompanying explanations that enable you to do just that - to appear as a leader that strikes confidence in everyone that, under your guidance, together, you will crack the trust code to ultimately build lasting relationships, navigate tough conversations with added ease, and foster this newly created extraordinary workplace build on diversity and inclusiveness that delivers beyond everyone's expectation and on everyone's satisfaction.

And there are only nine steps to achieve all of that even in the most hostile environment:

Step 1: Demonstration of knowledge and passion

You lead by example on one hand because employees predominantly assess your competence through your ability to execute their duties at least as equally good as they are. On the other, demonstrating superior skills acts enticing since you are setting a benchmark. The clear show of passion just adds to the overall positive experience; thus, solidifying your leadership status.

↓

Step 2: Setting clear and reasonable goals and expectations

By making sure you are staying in the realm of what's possible. Additionally, you should develop a habit to present goals in a visual form. And once you organize the work, ensure that every team member is familiar with the imposed expectation.

↓

Step 3: Trusting your team to deliver on those

Demonstrating the faith in their abilities even when things go sideways has a determining influence on your relationship with the team. They feel valued and trusted and thus, they feel responsible which creates a sense of obligation towards the entire group and not just you the manager. Each team member will invest additional efforts to avoid disappointment.

↓

Step 4: Acknowledging successes

As we've shown through the apple tree example and as several independent studies imply, if there is no direct social reward that validates the success, the effect is less than optimal and the lack of acknowledgment can even affect the learning curve. Add the fact that every employee, by default, yearns for the boss' approval and recognition, and you have a simple recipe for success. So do make sure to recognize and acknowledge each individual success.

↓

Step 5: Embracing failures and (collectively) learning from them

Trial and error is the only way we humans use in learning new skills. By setting optimized goals (breaking down complex goals to simpler milestones), you are ensuring that the mistake made a) doesn't endanger the entire project and b) turn into a valuable lesson for everyone.

↓

Step 6: Admitting own mistakes

The emphasis here is to acknowledge the consequence and offer a corrective set of actions rather than to just apologize. Such an approach is effectively transforming an error (in judgment, for example) into a new goal.

↓

Step 7: Sharing credit

This is done to validate the achievement on an individual or group level. In turn, this will incentivize a team member or the entire team to push even harder and ultimately reach a new level of commitment.

↓

Step 8: Keep cultivating the culture of diversity and inclusiveness

Whenever you find yourself in doubt about inclusiveness and/or diversity, remember the basic rule in physics: the opposites are attracting each other while the same reject one another. You can see this rule in almost every aspect of our existence; from the principle request of propagation that demands non-related; thus, diverse parents to learning new skills that solely depend on the diversity of inputs. In other words, you will learn more about the matter if you include different sources that even counter each other.

A homogenous environment is, by default, isolated from potentially valuable sources of knowledge. Hence, it is impaired in its ability to progress.

↓

Step 9: Continuous work on mastering conversations

The best way to excel in this vital skill is to practice it. That is to say, expose yourself to unpleasant and uncomfortable situations and engage in communication. If in doubt, consider the only efficient way to deal with fears and phobias.

But there is one thing that connects all these steps. What would you say is that one feature required to successfully pass each of these steps and ultimately build a high-trust organization?

What connects all the dots and is particularly important in the beginning?

Active Listening

Because just by hearing the others and validating their emotional states, standpoints, and expectations, you can create a clear image of the path ahead. The path that leads to improved teamwork, strong relationships, potent creativity, increased productivity, and, most importantly, the highest level of employees' engagement possible. This, in turn, gives birth to a supportive and diverse organization that not only delivers but serves as a role model.

Just like Stryker, one of the world's leading medical technology companies, where 95% of its almost 19,000 employees claim that they feel a sense of pride in what they have accomplished together and 94% say that they are proud to tell the others where they work. Or Accenture, a leading global professional services company, where **90% of employees report that they are willing to give extra to get the job done.**

And do you know what connects these two companies?

They were both named the Best Workplaces for Diversity™ in 2019. (Great Place to Work, 2019)

Yet another proof that the only true way to build a highly productive organization and prosper in your role as a manager is through trust, inclusiveness, and diversity.

And here, you have all the tools and guidance you need to build such an organization and put your life on a certain growth trajectory path.

Connect With the Author

Thank you for purchasing Building Trust for First-Time Manager. I cannot thank you enough for taking the time to read my work. If you found this book useful in any way, a review on Amazon would be immensely appreciated. For a new, independent author like myself, marketing is my biggest challenge, and your support makes a difference!

I read and respond to all my reader's questions. If you would like to reach out and get in touch with me, please email me at **phuang@successcirclehq.com**. I'm happy to connect!

Bibliography

Stanton, A. A., Day, M., & Welpe, I. M. (2010). *Neuroeconomics and the firm.* Northampton, MA, US: Edward Elgar Publishing.

A Brief History of Kodak. (n.d.). Retrieved from 1Ink.com: A Brief History of Kodak

Aaslaid, K. (2019). *50 EXAMPLES OF CORPORATIONS THAT FAILED TO INNOVATE.* Retrieved from Valuer: https://www.valuer.ai/blog/50-examples-of-corporations-that-failed-to-innovate-and-missed-their-chance

ADP. (2017, March 6). *3 Difficult Employee Conversations and How to Handle Them.* Retrieved from ADP: https://sbshrs.adpinfo.com/blog/3-difficult-employee-conversations-and-how-to-handle-them

American Psychological Association. (n.d.). Stress Effects on the Body. *APA.*

Apple. (2020). *Inclusion & Diversity.* Retrieved from Apple.com: https://www.apple.com/diversity/#:~:text=The%20next%20generation%20of%20leaders,employees%20from%202018%20to%2087.&text=Today%2C%2045%20percent%20of%20leaders,more%20representative%20than%20the%20last.

Apple Income Statement 2005-2020 | AAPL. (2020). Retrieved from Macrotrends: https://www.macrotrends.net/stocks/charts/AAPL/apple/income-statement

Artz, B., Goodall, A., & Oswald, A. (2015, January). Boss Competence and Worker Well-being. *Industrial and Labor Relations Review.* doi:10.1177/0019793916650451

Athene (Director). (2015). *Human Brain And Quantum Physics* [Motion Picture].

Banerjee, R., Reitz, J. G., & Oreopoulos, P. (2017). *DO LARGE EMPLOYERS TREAT RACIAL MINORITIES MORE FAIRLY? A NEW ANALYSIS OF CANADIAN FIELD EXPERIMENT DATA.* Toronto: University of Toronto.

Barends, E., Janssen, B., Velghe, C., Briner, R., & Rousseau, D. (2016). *Rapid evidence assessment of the research literature on the effect of goal setting on workplace performance.* Chartered Institute of Personnel and Development and Center for Evidence-Based Management. London: CIPD. Retrieved May 23, 2020, from https://www.cipd.co.uk/Images/rapid-evidence-assessment-of-the-research-literature-on-the-effect-of-goal-setting-on-workplace-performance_tcm18-16903.pdf

Blanchard, K., & Johnson, S. (2015). *One minute manager.*

Borges, P. (2017, June 13). *13 Consequences Of Not Setting Goals You Must Be Aware Of.* Retrieved May 23, 2020, from Motivate, Amaze, Be Great: https://www.

motivateamazebegreat.com/2017/06/13-consequences-of-not-setting-goals-you-must-be-aware-of.html

Bourke, J., & Dillon, B. (2018). The diversity and inclusion revolution: eight powerful truths. *Deloitte Review*.

Brown, S., Gray, D., McHardy, J., & Taylor, K. (2015). Employee trust and workplace performance. *Journal of Economic Behavior & Organization*, 361-378.

Buckingham, M. (2005). What Great Managers Do. *Harvard Business Review*.

Carter, C. (2015, November 12). *The Three Parts of an Effective Apology*. Retrieved from Greater Good Magazine: https://greatergood.berkeley.edu/article/item/the_three_parts_of_an_effective_apology

Clapham, W. (2010). *Breaking With the Law: The Story of Positive Tickets*. Richmond.CA: Amazon.

Conley, R. (2019, March 3). *Confronting Poor Performance is a "Moment of Trust" – 5 Steps for Success*. Retrieved from Leading with Trust: https://leadingwithtrust.com/category/challenging-conversations/

Credit Suisse Research Institute. (2012). *Gender Diversity and Corporate Performance*.

Cults, Explained (2019). [Motion Picture]. YouTube. Retrieved from https://www.youtube.com/watch?v=6NWIfiV1_XQ

Damasio, A. (2005). Brain trust. *nature*(435), 571-572. Retrieved May 21, 2020, from https://www.nature.com/articles/435571a

Dascal, L. (2018, April 13). *4 Impressive Ways Great Leaders Handle Their Mistakes*. Retrieved from Inc.: https://www.inc.com/lolly-daskal/4-impressive-ways-great-leaders-handle-their-mistakes.html

Deloitte. (2018). *Women and Minorities on Fortune 500 Boards: More Room to Grow*. Dohvaćeno iz The Wall Street Journal: https://deloitte.wsj.com/riskandcompliance/2019/03/12/women-and-minorities-on-fortune-500-boards-more-room-to-grow/

Deutsch, H. C. (2008). *At Kodak, Some Old Things Are New Again*. Retrieved from New York Times: https://www.nytimes.com/2008/05/02/technology/02kodak.html

Dhiraj, A. B. (2019, July 26). *These Are America's Top 10 Largest Companies By Revenue, 2019*. Retrieved from CEO World Magazine: https://ceoworld.biz/2019/07/26/these-are-americas-top-10-largest-companies-by-revenue-2019/

Dimoka, A. (2010, June). What Does the Brain Tell Us About Trust and Distrust? Evidence from a FunctionalNeuroimaging Study. *MIS Quarterly, 34*(2), pp. 373-396. Retrieved May 20, 2020, from https://www-jstor-org.libproxy.library.wmich.edu/stable/pdf/20721433.pdf?refreqid=excelsior%3A7e918dd12fdbf5d8b5f9b0ea023df732

Downey, S. N., Van Der Werff, L., Thomas, K. M., & Plaut, V. C. (2015). The role of diversity practices and inclusion in promoting trust and employee engagement. *Journal of Applied Social Psychology, 45*(1), 35-44.

Duhigg, C. (2012). *The Power of Habit: Why We Do What We Do in Life and Business.* New York: Random House.

Editorial. (n.d.). *5 Ways to Give Effective Praise to Motivate Your Team.* Retrieved from Lighthouse: https://getlighthouse.com/blog/ways-effective-praise-motivate-team/

Fine, G. A. (1998). *Morel Tales: The Culture of Mushrooming.* Cambridge, MA: Harvard University Press.

Froehlich, M. (2018, Januray 17). *Building Trust with Challenging Conversations.* Retrieved from Mandy Froehlich: https://mandyfroehlich.com/2018/01/17/building-trust-with-challenging-conversations/

go2HR. (2019). *UNDERSTANDING THE DIFFERENCES: LEADERSHIP VS. MANAGEMENT.* Retrieved January 16, 2020, from go2HR: https://www.go2hr.ca/retention-engagement/understanding-the-differences-leadership-vs-management

Golden, L., Henly, J., & Lambert, S. (2012). Work Schedule Flexibility: A Contributor to Employee Happiness? *Journal of Social Research and Policy.*

Great Place to Work. (2019). *Best Workplaces for Diversity ™ 2019.* Retrieved from Great PLace to Work: https://www.greatplacetowork.com/best-workplaces/diversity/2019

Griffin, C. (2019, July 3). *How Natural Black Hair at Work Became a Civil Rights Issue.* Retrieved from JSTOR Daily: https://daily.jstor.org/how-natural-black-hair-at-work-became-a-civil-rights-issue/

Gurchiek , K. (2019, March 19). *6 Steps for Building an Inclusive Workplace.* Retrieved from SHRM: https://www.shrm.org/hr-today/news/hr-magazine/0418/pages/6-steps-for-building-an-inclusive-workplace.aspx

Hagel, J., Seely Brown, J., Ranjan, A., & Byler, D. (2014). *Passion at work: Cultivating worker passion as a cornerstone of talent development.* Deloitte. Retrieved May 20, 2020, from https://www2.deloitte.com/us/en/insights/topics/talent/worker-passion-employee-behavior.html

Harkin, B., Webb, T. L., Chang P. I., B., Prestwich, A., Conner, M., Kellar, I., . . . Sheeran, P. (2016, February 19). Does Monitoring Goal Progress Promote Goal Attainment? A Meta-Analysis of the Experimental Evidence. *PubMed, 142*(2), 198-229. doi:10.1037/bul0000025

Harriss, L. (2019, July 30). *Six reasons it pays to trust your employees.* Retrieved from CIPHR: https://www.ciphr.com/features/six-reasons-trust-employees/

Heatfield, S. M. (2019, January 27). *What Great Managers Do Differently.* Retrieved January 17, 2020, from the balance careers: https://www.thebalancecareers.com/what-great-managers-do-differently-1918652

Hiraga, Y. (2005). British attitudes towards six varieties of English in the USA and Britain. *World Englishes, 24*(3), pp. 289-308.

Howe, C. H. (2012, January 30). *25 Warning Signs You Have a Low-Trust Organization.* Retrieved January 16, 2020, from Trusted Advisor: https://trustedadvisor.com/trustmatters/25-warning-signs-you-have-a-low-trust-organization-part-1-of-5

Kahneman, D. (2011). *Thinking, Fast and Slow.* New York: Farrar, Straus and Giroux.

Kennedy, S. (2018). *MANAGE A TOUGH CONVERSATION & BUILD TRUST.* Retrieved from Kennedy Spencer: https://kennedyspencer.net/manage-tough-conversation-build-trust/

Knight, R. (2015). How to Handle Difficult Conversations at Work. *Harvard Business Review.*

Kuhlmann, S., Piel, M., & Wolf, O. T. (2005). Impaired Memory Retrieval after Psychosocial Stress in Healthy Young Men. *The Journal of Neuroscience, 25*(11), 2977–2982. doi:10.1523/JNEUROSCI.5139-04.2005

Lattice. (2019, October 26). *How to Reduce Unconscious Bias at Work.* Retrieved from Lattice: https://lattice.com/library/how-to-reduce-unconscious-bias-at-work

Maxfield, M. (2018, August 17). *Seeing the Double-Slit Experiment for the First Time.* Retrieved from EEWeb: https://www.eeweb.com/profile/max-maxfield/articles/seeing-the-double-slit-experiment-for-the-first-time

MBN. (n.d.). *What is a manager? Definition and meaning.* Retrieved January 17, 2020, from Market Business News: https://marketbusinessnews.com/financial-glossary/manager-definition-meaning/

Morgan Stanley. (2016, May 11). *Why it pays to invest in gender diversity.* Retrieved from Morgan Stanley: https://www.morganstanley.com/ideas/gender-diversity-investment-framework.html

Moshtaghian, A., Croft, J., Murphy, P. P., McCleary, K., & Vera, A. (2020, June). *Atlanta officer who fatally shot Rayshard Brooks has been terminated.* Retrieved from CNN: https://edition.cnn.com/2020/06/13/us/atlanta-police-shooting-wendys/index.html

Murray, L. (n.d.). *Positive-sum game.* Retrieved from Encyclopaeida Britannica: https://www.britannica.com/topic/positive-sum-game#ref1189339

Nguyen, D. (2020, May 19). *Wave-Particle Duality.* Retrieved May 24, 2020, from LibreTexts: https://chem.libretexts.org/Bookshelves/Physical_and_Theoretical_Chemistry_Textbook_Maps/Supplemental_Modules_(Physical_and_Theoretical_Chemistry)/Quantum_Mechanics/09._The_Hydrogen_Atom/ Atomic_Theory/Electrons_in_Atoms/Wave-Particle_Duality

Nissen, E., Gunilla , L., Windström, A.-M., & Uvnás-Moberg, K. (1995). Elevation of oxytocin levels early post partum in women. *Acta Obstetricia et Gyne-cologica Scandinavica, 74*(7), 530-533.

Ohio State University. (2009). *Restoring Trust Harder When It Is Broken Early In Relationship.* ScienceDaily.

Oswald, A. J., Proto, E., & Sgroi, D. (2012). *Happiness and Productivity.* University of Warwick and IZA Bonn.

Parker, A. S., Lin, L., Clavel, C., Naha, C., Zlotnicka, E. T., & Alsford, J. (2016). *Putting Gender Diversity to Work: Better Fundamentals, Less Volatility.* New York: Morgan Stanley Global Quantitative Research.

Paulos, E. (2002). *Connexus.* Retrieved April 10, 2020, from www.paulos.net: http://www.paulos.net/research/intel/connexus/

Pillutla, M. M., Malhotra, D., & Murnighan, J. K. (2003). Attributions of trust and the calculus of reciprocity. *Journal of Experimental Social Psychology,* 448-455.

Polin, B., Lount, R. B., & Lewicki, R. J. (2018). On The Importance of a Full Apology: How to Best Repair Broken Trust. *Academy of Management.*

Qantas. (2017). *Qantas investor day 2017.* Qantas.

Redford, G. (2019, November 12). *Amy Edmondson: Psychological safety is critically important in medicine.* Retrieved from AAMC: https://www.aamc.org/news-insights/amy-edmondson-psychological-safety-critically-important-medicine

Reh, F. J. (2019, November 20). *Top Ten Myths About Managers.* Retrieved January 17, 2020, from the balance careers: https://www.thebalancecareers.-com/top-management-myths-2276189

Reinna, D., Reinna, M., & Hudnut, D. (2017). *Why trust is critical to team success.* Reinna. Retrieved May 21, 2020, from https://www.ccl.org/wp-content/up-loads/2017/05/why-trust-is-critical-team-success-research-report.pdf

Ringer, J. (n.d.). *We Have to Talk: A Step-By-Step Checklist for Difficult Conversations.* Retrieved from Judy Ringer: https://www.judyringer.com/resources/arti-cles/we-have-to-talk-a-stepbystep-checklist-for-difficult-conversations.php

Robison, J. (2006, November 9). *In Praise of Praising Your Employees.* Retrieved from Gallup: https://www.gallup.com/workplace/236951/praise-praising-employees.aspx

Roderick, M. K. (2009, June). Rethinking Trust. *Harvard Business review.*

Roland, S., & Blazer, M. A. (2019, January). Shared Knowledge and Verbal Communication in Football: Changes in Team Cognition Through Collective Training. *Frontiers in Psychology.* doi:DOI: 10.3389/fpsyg.2019.00077

Sawyer, P. J., Major, B., Casad, B. J., Townsend, S. S., & Berry Mendes, W. (2012). Discrimination and the Stress Response: Psychological and Physiological Consequences of Anticipating Prejudice in Interethnic Interactions. *American Journal of Public Health,* 1020-1026.

Schweitzer, M. E., Ordóñez, L., & Douma, B. (2017, November 30). Goal Setting as a Motivator of Unethical Behavior. *Academy of Management Journal, 47*(3). doi:10.5465/20159591

Scivicque, C. (2015, March). *Why Sharing Credit at Work Is Good For Your Career.* Retrieved from Eat Your Career: https://eatyourcareer.com/2015/03/why-sharing-credit-at-work-is-good-for-your-career/

Scott, M. (2015, July 29). *TOP 10 DIFFICULT CONVERSATIONS: NEW (SURPRISING) RESEARCH.* Retrieved from Chartered Management Institute: https://www.managers.org.uk/insights/news/2015/july/the-10-most-difficult-conversations-new-surprising-research

Sinek, S. (2009). *Start with Why: How Great Leaders Inspire Everyone to Take Action* (Vol. 1). New York: Portfolio.

SMART goals. (n.d.). Retrieved May 22, 2020, from Mind Tools: https://www.mindtools.com/pages/article/smart-goals.htm

Smith, M. M. (2015, August). *7 Ways Leaders Can Keep Their Promises (and the Trust) of Employees.* Retrieved from TLNT: https://www.tlnt.com/7-ways-leaders-can-keep-their-promises-and-the-trust-of-employees/

Staley, O. (2017, April). *Silicon Valley hires the most alumni of these 10 universities, and none of them are in the Ivy League.* Retrieved from QUARTZ: https://qz.com/967985/silicon-valley-companies-like-apple-aapl-hires-the-most-alumni-of-these-10-universities-and-none-of-them-are-in-the-ivy-league/

Sugawara, S. K., Tanaka, S., Okazaki, S., Watanabe, K., & Sadato, N. (2012). Social Rewards Enhance Offline Improvements in Motor Skill. *Plos One.*

(2016). *The Business Case for a High-Trust Culture.* New York: Great PLace to Work. Retrieved from https://s3.amazonaws.com/media.greatplacetowork.com/pdfs/Business+Case_Detailed+Report_Final.pdf

Thompson, J. (2013, November). *Active Listening Techniques of Hostage & Crisis Negotiators.* Retrieved from Psychology Today: https://www.psychologytoday.com/us/blog/beyond-words/201311/active-listening-techniques-hostage-crisis-negotiators

Todd, S. (2018, March 12). *A former Google engineer explains how creative freedom can turn people into entitled jerks.* Retrieved from Quartz: https://qz.com/work/1226761/a-former-google-engineer-explains-how-creative-freedom-can-turn-people-into-entitled-jerks/

Usborne, D. (2012). *The moment it all went wrong for Kodak.* Retrieved from Independent: https://www.independent.co.uk/news/business/analysis-and-features/the-moment-it-all-went-wrong-for-kodak-6292212.html

Van Edwards, V. (2016). *How to Build Trust With Anyone and Improve Your Relationships.* Retrieved May 21, 2020, from Science of People: https://www.scienceofpeople.com/build-trust/

Vanderbilt, U. (n.d.). *Unconscious Bias.* Retrieved from Vanderbilt University: https://www.vanderbilt.edu/diversity/unconscious-bias/

Wikipedia. (2020, June). *Killing of Rayshard Brooks*. Retrieved from Wikipedia: https://en.wikipedia.org/wiki/Killing_of_Rayshard_Brooks

Williams, J. C., & Mihaylo, S. (2019). How the Best Bosses Interrupt Bias on Their Teams. *Harvard Business review*.

Wilson, V. (2016). *People of color will be a majority of the American working class in 2032*. Economic Policy Institute.

Wired. (2009, February 24). 5 of the Worst Space Launch Failures. Retrieved May 19, 2020, from https://www.wired.com/2009/02/launchfailures/

World Bank. (2018). *Population, female (% of total population)*. Retrieved from World Bank: https://data.worldbank.org/indicator/SP.POP.TOTL.FE.ZS?end=2018&start=1960&view=chart

Zak, P. J. (January-February 2017). The Neuroscience of Trust: Management behaviors that foster employee engagement. *Harvard Business Review*.

Zak, P., & Knack, S. (2001). Trust and Growth. *Economic Journal, 111*(470), 295-321. Retrieved May 23, 2020, from https://econpapers.repec.org/article/ec-jeconjl/v_3a111_3ay_3a2001_3ai_3a470_3ap_3a295-321.htm

www.ingramcontent.com/pod-product-compliance
Lightning Source LLC
Chambersburg PA
CBHW071005120626
46546CB00003B/938